CW00762283

SPOOKY
New Orleans

SPOOKY
New Orleans

Tales of Hauntings, Strange Happenings,
and Other Local Lore

RETOLD BY S. E. SCHLOSSER

ILLUSTRATED BY PAUL G. HOFFMAN

Globe
Pequot

GUILFORD, CONNECTICUT

Globe
Pequot

An imprint of Rowman & Littlefield

Distributed by NATIONAL BOOK NETWORK

British Library Cataloguing in Publication Information available

Library of Congress Cataloging-in-Publication Data

Names: Schlosser, S. E., author. | Hoffman, Paul G., illustrator.
Title: Spooky New Orleans : tales of hauntings, strange happenings, and other local lore / retold by S.E. Schlosser ; illustrated by Paul G. Hoffman.
Description: Guilford, Connecticut : Globe Pequot, 2016. | Includes
   bibliographical references. | Description based on print version record
   and CIP data provided by publisher; resource not viewed.
Identifiers: LCCN 2016009175 (print) | LCCN 2015043020 (ebook) |
ISBN 9781493019199 (e-book) | ISBN 9781493019205 (pbk.)
Subjects: LCSH: Haunted places—Louisiana—New Orleans. |
 . Ghosts—Louisiana—New Orleans.
Classification: LCC BF1472.U6 (print) | LCC BF1472.U6 S3235 2016
(ebook) |
   DDC 398.209763/35—dc23
LC record available at http://lccn.loc.gov/2016009175

For Stacy Sullivan.
Thanks so much for sharing stories of your home.

For Lori Webster and Sue Evertt.
Thanks so much for making me part of the Fountain Hills family.

For my family: David, Dena, Tim, Arlene, Hannah, Emma,
Nathan, Ben, Deb, Gabe, Clare, Jack, Chris, Karen, Davey,
and Aunt Mil. And for my honorary sister, Barbara Strobel.

For all the wonderful folks at Globe Pequot, with my thanks.

Contents

INTRODUCTION   xi

PART ONE: GHOST STORIES

1.   *Counting Roses*   3
   ST. ROCH CEMETERY, NEW ORLEANS

2.   *Fatal Staircase*   7
   SAN FRANCISCO PLANTATION, GARYVILLE

3.   *Father Dagobert*   13
   ST. LOUIS CATHEDRAL, NEW ORLEANS

4.   *"Ave Maria"*   17
   A SHIP BOUND FOR NEW ORLEANS

5.   *Love Gone Awry*   23
   TOULOUSE STREET, NEW ORLEANS

6.   *The Myrtles*   27
   ST. FRANCISVILLE

7.   *Ghost on the Rooftop*   35
   ROYAL STREET, NEW ORLEANS

8.   *The Sausage Factory*   41
   NEW ORLEANS

9.   *Madame's Revenge*   47
   ST. ANN STREET

10.   *The Pirate's Ghost*   53
    LAFITTE'S BLACKSMITH SHOP

11.   *Un, Deux, Trois*   61
    BAYOU SEGNETTE

Contents

12.   *The Last Laugh*   65
      LAFAYETTE

13.   *The Specter's Treasure*   71
      BIENVILLE STREET, NEW ORLEANS

PART TWO: POWERS OF DARKNESS AND LIGHT

14.   *Preemptive Strike*   83
      ST. LOUIS CEMETERY NUMBER THREE, NEW ORLEANS

15.   *Shriveled Hearts*   89
      MISSISSIPPI RIVERFRONT, NEW ORLEANS

16.   *La Maison Mal*   95
      LALAURIE HOUSE, NEW ORLEANS

17.   *The Casquette Girls*   105
      URSULINE CONVENT, NEW ORLEANS

18.   *The Doctor*   113
      NEW ORLEANS PHARMACY MUSEUM

19.   *"Aidez-Moi"*   119
      LAKE PONTCHARTRAIN, NEW ORLEANS

20.   *Pool of Blood*   123
      CONSTANCE STREET, NEW ORLEANS

21.   *It's Just a Costume, Right?*   129
      BOURBON STREET, NEW ORLEANS

22.   *Forty-Nine Beaus*   135
      NEW ORLEANS

23.   *Mon Ami, Loup-Garou*   143
      GOVERNOR NICHOLLS STREET, NEW ORLEANS

24.   *The Death Tree*   149
      GARDETTE–LAPRETE HOUSE, NEW ORLEANS

Contents

25. *Voodoo Queen* 155
     LAVEAU HOUSE, NEW ORLEANS

26. *The Zombie* 165
     CHALMETTE BATTLEFIELD AND FORT ST. PHILIP

RESOURCES 174

ABOUT THE AUTHOR 179

ABOUT THE ILLUSTRATOR 180

Introduction

Davey stood motionless on the dock, staring at the man in the fancy white suit standing dramatically with one hand raised toward heaven and the other holding the leash of an invisible dog. Watching my nephew's face, I knew he was wondering: *Is he a statue, or is he real?*

Davey's stillness was noteworthy amid the hustle and bustle of the New Orleans waterfront. Tourists came chattering down the gangplank of the Steamboat *Natchez* docked directly behind us. Seagulls called and soared over the mighty Mississippi River. A jazz band played welcome home music in the park off to our right.

My sister tried not to laugh as she watched Davey struggle for meaning to the complex puzzle presented by the actor. "You can go closer if you want," she said.

I was watching the character actor, who kept his face perfectly still even though he must be squirming with delight inside. Apparently Davey's baffled expression was too much, even for him. Suddenly, the "statue" came to life and Davey gasped in astonishment. The actor walked over to us and recruited my nephew for his game. He set Davey up in the same dramatic pose—one hand raised toward the sky, one hand on the leash of the invisible dog. Then the actor joined him, mimicking my nephew flawlessly, right up to the look of confused delight on Davey's face. Passing tourists stopped to stare at man and boy.

Were they statues? Or were they real? My sister almost fell over, she laughed so hard.

Davey soon grew tired of the game, so we thanked the actor, gave him a big tip, and took my worn-out nephew to our hotel to have dinner and get some sleep. It was a fitting end to our first day in New Orleans.

What can I say about New Orleans that hasn't already been said a thousand times or more? The mysterious French Quarter with its narrow streets and colorful history was a delight to my eye and a source of keen interest to the folklorist in me. The ghost of Father Dagobert, the priest who defied the Spanish governor to see justice done, still walks the alley beside St. Louis Cathedral. The pirate Jean Lafitte haunts the old blacksmith shop he once used as a front for his smuggling business. As for the haunted LaLaurie house with its secret experiments . . . Well, I won't go into that here. There are some things you just have to experience for yourself ("La Maison Mal").

Marie Laveau, the famous Voodoo Queen, made her mark on New Orleans; as did General Andrew Jackson during the Battle of New Orleans ("The Zombie"). The supernatural community is also well represented in New Orleans. Tales of ghosts, vampires, *loup-garous*, and the deadly *coquin l'eau* abound in the region.

There are many reasons to visit New Orleans: Mardi Gras parades, the food, the culture, the history. But I promise you, what you will remember the most are the wonderful people— present and past—who have made New Orleans their home. I thank each and every one of them for making me feel so welcome south of the Salt Line.

—Sandy Schlosser

PART ONE
Ghost Stories

Counting Roses

ST. ROCH CEMETERY, NEW ORLEANS

There was a new fellow at church on Sunday. He was awkward as young men go, with too-big ears, a cowlick that wouldn't stay down, a goofy grin, and freckles across his nose. He reminded Carrie of a loose-limned scarecrow. The young man turned bright red and stammered when the reverend introduced them. His name was Jimmy, and he intrigued Carrie more than she cared to admit to her parents, who quizzed her about the young man over dinner.

On the third Sunday after they met, the youth asked if he could walk Carrie home after church. She accepted his invitation out of sheer curiosity. Would their walk be spent in silence, or would Jimmy muster the courage to talk to her? The invitation was the longest sentence he'd uttered in her presence.

To Carrie's surprise, Jimmy was quite erudite once he recovered a bit from the glory of her company. She found herself laughing until her sides ached. And many of his comments returned to her mind over the course of the next week. So she walked home with him again the next Sunday. And the next.

Soon her parents were inviting Jimmy to stay for Sunday dinner. Then he started dropping by the house after work on Tuesdays and Thursdays to play chess with her father and gape at Carrie when he thought she wasn't looking. Her parents gently teased her about her beau, but they liked Jimmy, even if he wasn't descended from New Orleans Creole aristocracy.

All of the New Orleans upper crust was invited to Carrie's come-out ball in October. Jimmy arrived in formal garb that looked strange on his lanky figure. He presented her with twenty-four white, red, and pink roses. "Can you guess their meaning?" he asked teasingly. Carrie did not guess correctly and was annoyed that her beau refused to tell her their meaning when they danced together at the ball. It was only when they parted for the night that Jimmy whispered in her ear: "A hint: The number of each rose corresponds to a letter in the alphabet."

Just before bed, Carrie counted the roses; nine white, twelve red, and three pink. ILC. What did it mean? Exasperating man! As she drifted to sleep, she suddenly realized that ILC meant "I love Carrie."

Jimmy proposed on Mardi Gras, going down on both knees and presenting her with a small diamond ring, which was all he could afford, though he swore he would earn a million dollars and cover her in jewels. Carrie didn't care. Her small diamond was enough.

Then Archduke Franz Ferdinand, heir to the Austro-Hungarian Empire, was shot to death by a Bosnian Serb nationalist in Sarajevo. Within weeks, a war to end all wars was declared in Europe. Jimmy enlisted in the American army when there was a call for volunteers, and she bravely watched him march away, her heart breaking.

Every week Carrie would write to her hero, and every week he would write to her, funny, cheerful letters with just the barest hint of the horrors he was encountering. Then a heart-stopping silence came; three weeks without a letter, followed by official notification of a terrible injury. They were sending Jimmy home to recover.

Carrie sat at the military hospital with Jimmy day and night, fighting for his life. But ultimately death claimed her betrothed. Carrie thought she would die, too, of a broken heart.

They buried Jimmy in the St. Roch Cemetery, and on his grave Carrie laid nine white, twelve red, and ten pink roses. ILJ. She also planted three small rosebushes—one of each color— beside his tombstone in memory of the night Jimmy first told her of his love.

Many months passed. Carrie visited Jimmy's grave each evening at dusk and talked about her day with her lost lover. But time heals even the brokenhearted. When a handsome young man came courting, Carrie started smiling again, if only faintly. The man could make her laugh a little, though not as Jimmy had. And he was rich and aristocratic and claimed to be Creole, though her parents had never heard of his family before he arrived in New Orleans. Still, it was deemed a good match, if only Carrie could reconcile her heart to this newcomer.

The day came when the young aristocrat proposed marriage to Carrie. She liked him well enough, but her heart was still buried with Jimmy. Her parents wished her to marry this man, but Carrie was not so sure. Her instinct told her that something wasn't right, though she had no reason to doubt him.

Carrie begged for twenty-four hours to think about it, and the young man graciously consented to the delay. He swaggered away, already sure of her answer. His cocky manner irritated Carrie. She threw a cloak over her dress, for it was the coldest part of winter, and went to St. Roch Cemetery to sit beside Jimmy's tombstone.

"I don't know if you can hear me, Jimmy," Carrie said, a tear rolling down her cheek. "I miss you so much, and I need your advice. There is a young Creole man who wants to marry me, and Papa approves of the match. But my heart still belongs to you, and I don't know how to answer him. Please, love, please send me a sign."

Carrie buried her face in her hands, overcome by frustration and fatigue. Suddenly, a warm breeze caressed her cheek like the touch of a hand. Carrie looked up and saw that two of the rosebushes were full of blossoms where none had been a moment before. Slowly, she plucked them one by one. There were fourteen red buds and fifteen white buds. N.O. Carrie gasped and burst into tears of relief. Jimmy wanted her to refuse the proposal! She would not go against the wishes of the dead. "Thank you, love," she whispered, pressing the flowers against her wet cheek.

The aristocrat was incredibly rude when she refused his proposal. In the end, her father threw him out of the house and forbade his return. Two days later, their neighbor came around with shocking news. The young aristocrat had just been arrested by the New Orleans police. It seemed he was wanted for bigamy . . . and for murder. The young aristocrat had married two different Creole girls from wealthy families and then killed them after they made wills in his favor.

Carrie's mother fainted when she heard this news and her father clutched his heart, ashamed that he'd urged his only child to marry such a brute. Carrie picked up the vase of red and white roses from its place of honor on the table and whispered a thank-you to her beloved Jimmy, who was still taking care of her from beyond the grave.

2

Fatal Staircase

It was the last day but one of our Louisiana trip, and we woke to a sparkling morning full of sunshine and promise. After a leisurely breakfast, our travels took us downriver to tour the San Francisco plantation near New Orleans.

As we drove down the road, my sister Karen told us the history of the Steamboat Gothic plantation home. According to the literature, Edmond Bozonier Marmillion built the mansion along the Mississippi River but did not live long enough to enjoy it. He died suddenly, shortly after he completed the home, and the plantation was inherited by his sons.

Valsin, the elder son, married a German woman named Louise, who spent a fortune lavishly decorating the new mansion. Creoles in the area jokingly called the house "Sans Fruschin," an expression that means "without a penny," because of the high cost of the furnishings. The house was later renamed San Francisco Plantation, as it remains to this day.

The two sons, Charles and Valsin Marmillion, managed to survive the post–Civil War economy and grew a successful sugarcane business. Sadly, the two brothers died young, within a few years of each other. Valsin's German bride sold

7

the plantation in 1879 and returned to Europe with her three daughters.

As Karen finished reading the story in the brochure, I saw the sign for the plantation and turned into the parking lot. We exited the car and went toward the entrance gate. I could see the fancy painted mansion rising up from a beautifully kept lawn. The house looked like a layered birthday cake. It was a lovely scene, but for some reason to me the mansion felt lonely and desolate, as if it had been abandoned.

I followed my sister and nephew through the entrance gate and recoiled as soon as I set foot on the property. The air around the plantation felt dark and slimy. I rubbed my suddenly cold arms; my stomach was roiling with sudden nausea. Good Lord, what was wrong with this place? I glanced ahead. My sister and nephew were waiting for me to catch up. Reluctantly, I forced myself forward. It felt like I was walking through thick molasses as I crossed the garden to join them.

When I reached Karen, my psychic sister glanced from me to the mansion and nodded, silently confirming the fact that the plantation was haunted.

"I know," I whispered, hoping that Davey wouldn't hear me. My nephew was a bit young for ghost hunting, although his sixth sense was as strong as his mother's. "I don't like this place at all. Do you think we should take him in?" I nodded toward Davey.

"It's probably all right," Karen said. "Anyway, we're here now, so let's take the tour."

I felt a bit dubious, but she was the mom, so I went with her decision.

We entered the gift shop to purchase tickets. I lingered among the books and toys as long as I could, but soon we were walking along the path that led to the house. I wanted to run away, but Karen and Davey went inside, so I followed them. It took an act of courage to step over the threshold. As soon as I entered the mansion, I felt the heavy presence of a ghost on the upper floor. Yikes.

A friendly woman in period garb greeted us and smiled sweetly at my cute little nephew as I drew several deep breaths for control. Concerned, I glanced at Davey to see how he was responding to the house, but he seemed okay. Karen wasn't okay. She'd gone very pale and kept glancing uneasily around the room. My sister is clairvoyant. I wondered if she was seeing a different, older version of the house than the one in which we currently stood.

To me, the mansion felt worn out, and I sensed something evil lurking in the walls. I don't know how the tour guides could stand it. The only way I was going make it through this house was to shield my sixth sense as strongly as I could. Ye gods, let this be a fast tour.

My sister drew the guide into a discussion of the paranormal. The guide told us some of the folktales that were circulating about the plantation. According to the stories, visitors and guides alike have encountered the figure of a man in various rooms; particularly in the younger son Charles's room upstairs. One tour guide said she saw a man staring at her through an outside window. At first, the guide thought the man must be a curious tourist. Then she realized she was standing on the second floor of the plantation house and that the man gazing through the glass was floating in midair!

Little Davey guffawed when he heard that story, a reassuring sound. I only wish it made me feel better about this haunted place. As we talked, the tour guide escorted us through the kitchen and the storage rooms. I gazed in fascination at several large jars that were sunk into the brick floor, where workers could put perishable food to keep it cool.

We entered a room with a long steep staircase at one end. As soon as I saw it, I stopped with a gasp. Something terrible had happened here. Overwhelmed by a sense of dread, I fought to keep my breakfast down as the air darkened around me like a cloud covering the sun. I heard a faint buzzing in my ears, and then someone screamed in fear. For a split second, I saw a small body toppling down the steps, skirts flapping wildly. It vanished in a heartbeat, and I stood frozen in horror, staring at the empty staircase.

The guide herself had no hesitation in climbing the haunted staircase, and Davey followed on her heels. Like me, Karen was staring at the stairs in horror, as if she sensed that something bad had happened on the stairs. Motherhood propelled her up the stairs after her son, but I could see she was trying to get up the steps as fast as she could.

Last in line, I hesitated at the base of the stairs. "I am so sorry," I murmured aloud to the little figure I'd seen falling down this steep stairwell. Then I grabbed the railing with trembling hands and walked up to the second floor. By the time I reached the top step, I felt feverish and ill with stress.

We walked through one incredibly gorgeous room after the next. Influenced by Louise's German heritage, the rooms burst with vivid colors, hand-painted ceilings, and period antiques.

Everywhere I looked, I saw hand-carved trim and the lavish use of faux wood-grain painting.

Everywhere I walked, I sensed an invisible man with a cigar wandering about the rooms.

There was something else, something darker, that lurked in the background of this lavishly decorated plantation house. I had no idea who or what it was, but I didn't like it one bit.

When we reached the boudoir at the center of the house, my nephew grew restless and wouldn't stay in the room for more than a moment. I couldn't blame him. The room was suffocating. I sensed a dying child; a woman's terrible grief. My mind flashed back to the little girl falling helplessly down the stairs. I blocked the memory and focused my attention on the tour guide, hoping to heaven that we could get out of this room as quickly as possible.

When we finally stepped across the hallway and into the next set of rooms, I found Karen standing motionless in the doorway of a small study that seethed with a cold, restless breeze. She stared wide-eyed at the ledger on the desk as the tour guide swept past her. The woman's presence broke my sister's trance. Karen blinked as if she'd suddenly stepped into the sunlight and then shook her head as if to clear it.

"What did you see?" I whispered to her.

"There was a man in a blue velvet coat sitting at the desk chair, paging through his ledger," she replied.

We were at the end of our tour—thank God—and I couldn't wait to get out of this haunted house. But our tour guide had taken a fancy to us and wanted to tell us more stories about the supernatural. To my chagrin, we were hauled downstairs for a final supernatural discussion instead of escaping through the front door, which was customary. When Karen asked about the staircase, the tour guide told her that a little girl had fallen to her death down the steps. "Most people believe it was this steep inside staircase, though a few claim that it was the grand staircase at the main entrance," she said. "There have been reports of people being scratched on this staircase as they walk up to the second floor."

Eventually, Karen managed to stem the tide of storytelling and get us out of the mansion. The guide pressed a lovely souvenir book upon us as a farewell gift. I think she paid for it with her own money. Karen thanked her and we finally (finally!) limped off the grounds as fast as humanly possible, glad to leave this haunted spot behind.

"Did you see the man watching us from the top of that long staircase?" Karen asked me quietly as Davey trotted across the lawn toward the entrance.

"No," I replied shortly. "I saw the little girl falling down it."

Davey skipped back to us at this juncture, effectively ending our conversation. Thank goodness. I'd had about as much as I could take.

The slimy feeling followed us the rest of the morning. Just before noon, I stopped the car and we threw away every last piece of documentation we had about the plantation, including the souvenir book that we were given by the guide. This action convinced whatever negative vibration that was haunting us that we seriously wished to be left alone. Once the literature was out of the car, the nasty feeling finally abated.

As I returned to the car, I noticed a long scratch on the bottom of my right arm. Was that scratch on my arm before we arrived at the mansion this morning, or did I get it while we toured the house? I shuddered. I didn't want to know the answer.

I got back into the car and told Karen that I was never going to set foot in San Francisco Plantation ever again.

"Me, neither," my sister replied.

3

Father Dagobert

ST. LOUIS CATHEDRAL, NEW ORLEANS

It was too much: The constant weeping and wailing of her mother- and sister-in-laws; the well-meaning but cruel platitudes of the church members; the complaints from her parents. "Why did you marry such a daredevil?" her mother cried. "A tragedy was bound to happen."

Through some ironic twist of fate, Henri, her "daredevil" husband, was not killed during some foolish prank or wild horse race, as her parents once predicted. No, he died when a drunken man smashed his newfangled automobile into Henri's carriage while her husband was driving home from an appointment outside of town.

The young widow slipped away from the house where the mourners gathered to view Henri's body in the simple casket. The funeral was on the morrow, but the young widow believed the funeral and the supper to follow would be more of a sad carnival than a time to mourn her beloved. So she walked through a drizzling rain toward St. Louis Cathedral where Mass would be said for her beloved husband, mourning alone. She felt too numb even to weep.

Oh Henri. *Henri.* Her heart wrung inside her chest, and the young widow hugged her arms around her middle. Here was yet another irony: that a person truly could writhe in agony. Who knew the body would react so severely to mental torment? She staggered and almost fell, catching hold of an iron lamppost at the last moment to keep upright. If only she had been in the carriage with Henri, they might have died together and she would have been spared this terrible pain.

The cathedral loomed before her in the dusk, and the young widow touched the rain-damp wall as she limped painfully forward, afraid that she would lose her balance once more. She stopped abruptly, heart pounding, when she realized where her subconscious mind had brought her. It was here, in this tiny alley by the cathedral, that Henri had proposed marriage to her. Right on this spot.

"Sainte Marie, Mère de Dieu," she gasped and fell to her knees in the rain, weeping.

She was roused from her grief by a deep baritone voice singing softly: "Kyrie, eleison! Christe, eleison! Kyrie, eleison!"

The young widow looked up and saw a priest in a simple brown robe walking slowly down the alley, hands folded in prayer. He sang softly as he paced beside the large cathedral wall. She gasped and wiped her eyes, ashamed at being found crumpled in the street like a lowly beggar. What must the Father think of her? She tried to stand, but her legs would not hold her. She sank back onto her knees and buried her face in her hands in sudden despair.

A moment later, she felt the priest's hand on her shoulder. He murmured: "Take heart, my daughter. This is a great loss, I know. Henri's death came too soon, as did the deaths of six Frenchmen so long ago. I will say Mass for your husband tomorrow, and I will grieve with you. But remember that you will be reunited with Henri someday in heaven."

The young widow looked intently at the priest standing over her in the rain-soaked darkness. His face glowed as if it was a reflection of heaven's eternal light. She reached up a trembling hand, and he took it. "Do not be afraid, my daughter," the priest said. And vanished before her eyes.

The young widow gasped. "Father! Where are you?" And then she realized what had happened. She had just spoken with the ghost of Father Dagobert!

Father Dagobert was the bishop of St. Louis Church back in 1769 when the Spanish came to New Orleans, determined to squash the insurrection of the French colonists. Governor O'Reilly routed the resistance in short order and executed six of the Creole leaders as a deterrent to the rest of the rebels. By the new governor's orders, the men's bodies were left on display to rot on the drilling grounds of the levee. Father Dagobert was appalled. The executed men had attended his church for years and deserved a decent burial. And their families deserved a proper mourning period for their dead. The widows of the dead men appealed to the governor, to no avail. So Father Dagobert and his followers slipped out one dark night past the guards on duty and retrieved the bodies of the executed rebels. By some miracle of God, they were neither seen nor heard as they went about their mission of mercy. When they returned to the church, Father Dagobert said a funeral Mass for the dead Creole rebels. Then the bodies were interred in Cemetery Number One.

The young widow should have been frightened by her ghostly encounter, but instead it gave her heart. Father Dagobert had promised to say Mass with them tomorrow. And he said she would one day be reunited with her beloved Henri. Who was she to question a message from heaven?

The young widow stood between her father and her mother-in-law the next morning in St. Louis Cathedral while the priest said Mass for Henri. From the balcony, the young widow heard a persistent echo, as if another voice was speaking the Mass in time with his modern-day counterpart. When the final amen was spoken, a baritone voice rang out over the congregation: "In paradisum deducant angeli; in tuo adventu suscipiant te martyrus et perducant te in civitatem sanctam Jerusalem." (May the angels lead you into paradise; at your coming may the martyrs receive you and lead you to the holy city of Jerusalem.)

The congregation gasped and looked up. For a moment, the glowing outline of a Capuchin monk—Father Dagobert— appeared before them. Then he was gone.

4

"Ave Maria"

A SHIP BOUND FOR NEW ORLEANS

It was the fault of the woman, Dane decided dispassionately as he brooded in his quarters. He was a good ship captain and an honest man. At least he had been, until the day the young and lovely Julia Regalea came aboard his ship bearing trunks full of money and jewels, a beautiful harp, and a much-older husband. The couple had fled the revolution in their South American country and hoped to start a new life in New Orleans. Dane could hardly take his eyes off the woman walking up the gangplank, and she was equally fixated upon him. Her husband, who was elderly and a complainer, did not notice their mutual attraction.

In the days that followed, Dane found every opportunity to mix with his wealthy passengers. Each night, they dined with him at the captain's table. Most evenings, the elderly husband drank too much wine and fell asleep in his chair, leaving the pair unwatched. One night, a storm churned up the sea. Seeing his chance, Dane lured the old man on deck after dinner and pushed him overboard when a convenient wave slapped across the hull, drenching the ship. And suddenly Julia was a rich widow with no encumbrances. At least, no visible ones. Too late, Dane discovered the one major drawback in this lovely woman. She had a conscience.

The love affair turned sour. Julia Regalea agreed to marry Dane if he went with her to confession when they reached New Orleans. Having got away with murder, Dane had no intention of confessing to a priest, and so he told Julia in no uncertain terms. After their argument, Julia stayed in her cabin and played hymns sadly upon her harp, hoping the music would work on his conscience where words could not.

In a way, her plan succeeded. Dane felt guilty every time he went on deck and saw the place where he pushed the elderly husband overboard. Worse, his crew suspected something. The storm had not been wild. It was not the sort of storm to take a life, unless that person had very bad luck. Or if the person happened to be a rich, elderly man with a beautiful wife who was having an affair with the captain. None of the sailors voiced their suspicions aloud. But Dane saw the men whispering in corners and watching him. And so Dane retreated to his quarters to concoct an evil plan.

Just a night shy of their destination, the crew anchored offshore in the gulf and Dane hosted a party for crew and passengers. Much ale and wine was consumed, and the merrymakers did not observe the five sailors busily loading trunks full of gold and jewels into a small boat. Nor did they smell the smoke as the men set fire to the ship. In his cabin, the captain raised a wineglass to Julia Regalea and his officers in a mocking salute and then deliberately left them in the room and climbed down the side of the ship to the waiting rowboat.

Dane and his five sailors were well under way when the drunken crew discovered hot flames engulfing the sails. As they pulled for shore, the men in the rowboat heard the lovely sound of a harp playing "Ave Maria" as the ship burned. For a moment, Dane and his men stopped rowing. Then a small wave jostled the boat. Dane's foot struck a chest full of gold and jewels they had stolen from Julia Regalea and her dead husband, and his face hardened with greed. He snapped out an order, and the rowing resumed in the lurid glaring light of the fiery vessel. Dane and his men had just landed on the far shore when fire reached the ammunition hold and the mighty ship exploded, killing everyone on board. The shock wave knocked them off their feet. Debris cascaded everywhere. The deed was done.

The sailors buried the treasure chests at the foot of a large oak tree and then stumbled into the local community to present themselves as refugees from a tragic accident. Their story was believed. A friendly landowner drove the captain and his men into New Orleans, where they were met with such hospitality and friendship that Dane decided to stay. He purchased a grand house with the money from one of the Regalea trunks and lived a life of ease in the company of his fellow survivors.

Nearly a year passed in leisure and enjoyment for the supposed refugees. During his sojourn, Dane wooed the lovely daughter of a Creole aristocrat who lived in the neighborhood and won her love in return. But the engagement foundered when the woman discovered that Dane did not attend Mass. After much pleading, Dane agreed to accompany his betrothed to church one evening in midsummer. Alas for his sweetheart, one of the first hymns played in the service was "Ave Maria." Dane turned white as a sheet when he heard the music. He left the service abruptly, swearing never to set foot in the church again. Furious and embarrassed by his behavior, the aristocrat's daughter broke their engagement.

Then yellow fever swept through New Orleans. All the members of Dane's household fell ill. Dane shook off the disease with ease, but his men did not fare so well. One by one, the sailors perished of the disease, until only one man remained. On his deathbed, he confessed everything to his nurse, who was a simple woman much given to embroidering the truth. When she repeated the sailor's tale of murder, stolen treasure, and a burned ship, the good folks of New Orleans put it down to daftness and old age. But there was a perceptible difference in the way Dane was treated by his neighbors once the rumor spread abroad.

Dane was frightened. He didn't think there was any proof to support the accusations leveled against him by the dying sailor. But he could not be sure. Deciding it was time to flee, Dane packed his bags and stole off in the night. He drove a wagon toward the shore where the remaining trunks of treasure lay buried beneath the oak tree. Unbeknownst to Dane, he arrived at the burial spot on the very anniversary of the burning of his merchant ship and plunged his shovel into the dirt in the same hour that—one year ago—he had saluted his former lover and left her to die aboard his ship.

Dane dug in darkness, kept company only by the sound of the restless hissing waves on the shore. Suddenly, a garish light flared in the gulf, blazing a sickly red-orange path across the moaning sea. Dane whirled in fright, raising his shovel like a weapon. Across the bay, a merchant ship burned gruesomely, flames licking the masts and sails. Fire poured from every porthole. Then the music began, wailing harp music pitched so high it made Dane's hair stand on end. The song was a malevolent parody of "Ave Maria."

As Dane watched in horror, a boat was lowered from the burning ship and many flaming men climbed down and swung themselves into the vessel. The burning sailors rowed to the beat of the mocking "Ave Maria," moving with supernatural speed. Blue light flared around them, illuminating the faces of the corpses within the small vessel. Burned and blackened, skin ripped to tatters by the blast, the specters were still recognizable. Each was a member of Dane's dead crew.

Heart pounding wildly and cold sweat pouring down his face, Dane leaped backward in revulsion and fear as the boat landed on the sand and the burning corpses rushed ashore. Dane held up his shovel—a meager weapon against so deadly a foe—and screamed: "I didn't mean to do it! It was the fault of the woman!" The specters overwhelmed him before he could strike a single blow.

The next morning, an early riser digging for clams came across the broken and burnt body of Dane lying in a heap of gold and jewels under a large oak tree. Beside him stood a water-stained, seaweed-strewn harp.

5

Love Gone Awry

Mary waited in the parlor, pacing furiously back and forth. She had decided to confront her errant third husband when he got home that evening about the woman he was keeping as his mistress.

Twice widowed, Mary had married a handsome Frenchman named Joseph Baptandiere and brought him to live in her beautiful brick home in New Orleans. At first, all was bliss between them. He was courtly and well mannered, respectful and well spoken. His manner toward his wife was irreproachable (and he wasn't a bad kisser, either, though she naturally would never discuss this aspect of their relationship with her very respectable friends).

As time went on, she realized that something was missing from their relationship. He was always courtly and respectful, but the gleam that she'd seen in his dark eyes at the beginning of their courtship had faded some time ago. He carried out his husbandly duties, but his enthusiasm had waned.

Little clues came her way, one at a time. Friends would stop gossiping when she walked into a room. Servants would eye her knowingly and shake their heads. Neighbors spoke to her in a pitying tone she found maddening. What did they know about Joseph Baptandiere that she did not?

A little investigation revealed the truth, and it stunned her into immobility for a time. Joseph's heart had been swept away by a dark-haired beauty named Angelique shortly after their marriage, and they had set up a *plaçage* together. Plaçage was considered a "left-handed marriage" in which a man set up a separate household for his mistress. Joseph's mistress, Angelique, lived in a lovely house on Rue de Rampart with servants to care for her every need. Plaçage was a practice Mary despised, and now she—Joseph's legal wife—was its latest victim. No wonder the neighbors pitied her.

Worse still was the rumor that Angelique wanted more than a plaçage. According to the grocer's wife, Angelique loved Joseph madly and wished him to divorce Mary and marry her instead. It was the topic of frequent arguments between them. So far, Joseph was standing—admittedly in a rather wobbly way—behind his marriage vows. But who knew for how long? Mary would not countenance a divorce. Think of the scandal! As soon as Joseph returned home, she would tell him the jig was up. He would have to part with Angelique or lose all the money his wealthy wife used to sustain him.

The hour grew late and still there was no sign of Joseph. Mary's fury turned to unease. She went to the bellpull, but before she could ring it a frantic servant boy burst into the room.

"Oh, Mistress! Oh, Mistress," he sobbed. "He was burying her in the yard out back. I saw him with my own eyes, Mistress."

"What?" Mary gasped. "Who was burying whom in the backyard? Calm down and tell me exactly what you saw," she demanded, wringing her hands.

"I was gazing out the window on the fourth floor, and I saw the Master in the courtyard," the boy panted, dark eyes wide with horror. "He had a body next to him. It was his *placée*, the woman Angelique. I think he strangled her to death, Mistress! There were marks on her neck. I watched him throw her body into the sewage well. Oh, Mistress." The boy broke down crying, and Mary fetched him a glass of water from a pitcher on the sideboard.

"Where is the Master now?" she inquired grimly.

"I don't know, Mistress," the boy said after gulping down several mouthfuls of water. "He saw me and ran away. The placée is still out there in the hole. Her neck was all bruised and her dead eyes stared up at me in horror. . . ." The glass fell from his shaking hands, and he rocked back and forth in grief.

At that moment, Mary heard a thud and a muffled scream from the direction of the courtyard. "Someone must have found the body," Mary said. She told the servant boy to stay in the parlor and hastened out to the yard. Servants were milling about and pointing upward in shock and revilement. Mary looked toward the roof and swayed in horror. The body of her husband Joseph swung from a rope hanging out of the third-floor window, face contorted in death and limbs still twitching.

"*Mais non, mon Dieu,*" Mary screamed.

Right behind the shock came a feeling of outrage. How could he do this to her, his legal wife? What a terrible scandal. It would be the talk of New Orleans. The placée murdered and now her husband taking his own life in remorse. What would the neighbors say?

The murder-suicide was the talk of the town for months. The scandal was just beginning to fade from collective memory when a new twist in the plot revived the story. The apparition of the fair Angelique began materializing on the third floor of the brick house every evening at dusk. The ghost would mournfully watch the servants as they bustled about the business of the household. Sometimes the lovely Angelique would stare through the window where her dead lover hanged himself. Whenever she gazed through the windowpane, the ghost of Joseph appeared, dead body dangling from a rope. Observers could hear his corpse thumping softly against the house with the slightest touch of the nighttime breeze.

Mary's neighbors were scandalized the first time Joseph's ghost appeared hanging from the roof. The appearance of the ghosts revived the story of the older scandal, and once again Mary was embarrassed before New Orleans' high society. For a time, she contemplated selling the house and moving someplace where the story was not so well known. But then, Mary reasoned, her wayward husband would have cuckolded her once again, this time from beyond the grave. So Mary firmed her lips, lifted her chin, and remained in the ghost house.

Who would have guessed, she thought bitterly, that her final years would be tangled up in a ghostly love triangle? After the servants went to bed that night, Mary went up to the third floor and threw shoes at Angelique's mournful apparition to relieve her feelings. This had no effect on the mournful ghost and her swinging paramour, but it made Mary feel better.

Mary stuck it out for ten years. She died in 1817 and the haunted house passed to her heirs. But the ghosts of Angelique and Joseph remained in the brick house on Toulouse Street long after Mary was gone—a poignant reminder of what happens when love goes awry.

6

The Myrtles

ST. FRANCISVILLE

The most haunted house in America. That's what all the publicity proclaimed about the Myrtles. Which made it irresistible for a folklore enthusiast such as myself. What better way to spend an evening than taking a tour of a haunted house, deep in the interior of Louisiana? It was a hard sell to my husband, the nonbeliever. He thought ghosts were rubbish and took delight in repeating his opinions to everyone he met. But every marriage comes with some trials, and Harry's nonbelief was mine.

"It's a historical house," I told Harry over lunch. "It was built in 1796 by General David Bradford—you probably know him as Whiskey Dave of the Whiskey Rebellion. Anyway, he fled the United States for the Louisiana colony to avoid arrest and imprisonment. He obtained a land grant of 650 acres from the Baron de Corondelet and had this house built on what is now known to be an Indian burial ground."

"Huh," my husband said, sipping thoughtfully at his diet soda. Harry loved history, and I'd heard him discussing the Whiskey Rebellion at length with his cronies.

My ploy worked. Harry decided that we should have dinner in the Carriage House Restaurant at the Myrtles and then take a tour of the house. Score one for the folklorist, I thought, but knew better than to say so aloud.

What I'd neglected to tell Harry was the rest of the Myrtles story: the legend that gave the house its haunted reputation. According to the tale, the Myrtles was sold in 1820 to Judge Clarke Woodruff, who was Whiskey Dave's son-in-law. The judge expanded and remodeled the mansion and settled there with his wife, Sarah Matilda, and their children. Sarah gave birth to several children, and the family lived there in happiness and prosperity until an event took place that still haunts the Myrtles today.

A house slave named Chloe who was allegedly having an affair with her master became frightened that she would lose her place in the household and be sent instead to the brutal hard work of the fields. Hoping to discover their plans for her future, Chloe eavesdropped on the Woodruff family's most private conversations, hiding herself in corners and lurking under open windows long after she'd been dismissed from the room. One day, the judge caught her eavesdropping and ordered one of her ears cut off to teach her a lesson. Humiliated by her disfiguration, Chloe began wearing a green turban around her head to hide the ugly scar that the knife had left behind.

Determined to reinstate herself with the judge and his family, Chloe came up with a plan. She would put oleander poison into a birthday cake for the oldest daughter's party—just a little bit to make the family fall ill. Then she would nurse them back to health. The judge and his family would be so grateful that they would guarantee her a permanent place on the house's staff, rather than sending her to work in the fields. But Chloe's plan backfired. She put too much poison in the cake batter. Sarah and two of her children fell ill immediately and died within a few hours.

The judge, who had not eaten any cake, survived.

When the facts about the poisoning became known, the plantation slaves dragged Chloe from the house and hanged her from a nearby tree. Then her body was cut down, weighted with rocks, and thrown into the river.

After the funeral Woodruff closed off the children's dining room, where the party was held, and never used it again as long as he lived. Tragically, Woodruff's life was also cut short a few years later by a murderer.

The ghost of Chloe has frequently been reported wandering the grounds of the Myrtles plantation, wearing a green turban to hide her cut-off ear. In fact, Chloe's unhappy spirit was once photographed by a past owner of the Myrtles plantation. The owner was documenting the exterior of the Myrtles to aid the underwriters in rating a fire insurance policy for the plantation, and found an anomaly in one of the photographs taken near the house. A ghostly slave girl, thought to be Chloe, appeared standing in the breezeway between the General's Store and the Butler's Pantry of the mansion. The boards of the mansion house were clearly visible through her body. Apparently, the plantation sold the picture as a postcard souvenir. I was determined to purchase one during our visit, though I wasn't sure if I'd show it to Harry.

We drove to the Myrtles in the early evening. I was breathless with excitement as we pulled into the long driveway in our vacation rental car. Would I see a translucent antebellum woman sweeping up the front steps or ghostly children playing in the garden? Or maybe Chloe in her green turban would be standing beneath the hanging tree! Instead, what unfolded before my eyes was a white mansion with a long veranda, ornamental ironwork, and large rocking chairs to either side of the front steps. The house was surrounded by centuries-old live oak trees.

To all outward appearances, the scene before me was one of peaceful serenity, bathed in the golden light of late afternoon. But the sight of that lovely house made my arms prickle with goose bumps. I swallowed nervously, my throat suddenly dry. Oh my goodness! There wasn't any doubt in my mind that this plantation house was haunted.

Beside me, my pragmatic spouse grunted: "Pretty place. I wonder if this was the original building Whiskey Dave built or if they added a couple of additions."

Harry parked the car and then asked: "So, what should we do first? Dinner or house tour?"

I took a calming breath and said: "Let's get tickets for the tour and see if there's time for dinner beforehand."

"Good idea," Harry said. He took my hand as we strolled toward the house and snuggled me close to him with a kiss to my forehead. Harry might be annoyingly pragmatic about the paranormal, but I wouldn't trade my husband for anyone else.

I was very glad that Harry had joined me for this excursion. I could feel someone watching us from the upstairs window of the mansion. But when I looked, there was nobody there; at least, there was nobody visible. Chills ran through my body, and Harry felt me shiver. "Do you need your sweater from the car?" he asked me.

"No, I'm all right," I replied. After all, it had been my idea to visit the Most Haunted House in America. I shouldn't be surprised to sense spirits here.

We got tickets from the gift shop and found we had just enough time to stroll the grounds before the next tour began.

"We'll eat dinner after the tour," Harry said, pocketing the tickets and reclaiming my hand.

The grounds were smaller than I'd expected, but there were lovely views from all sides of the mansion. Then we walked around the rental cabins, wondering if we should stay in one of them on our next trip.

My favorite discovery was a small pond with a bridge leading to an island gazebo. Frogs trilled a buzzing chorus all around the small island. It felt cozy and spooky, all at once. I wondered if the ghost of the Native American woman that was sometimes seen on the grounds haunted this lovely place. I didn't repeat my speculations to Harry, who was trying to remember the scientific name of the small frogs singing in the bulrushes.

"Time for our tour," Harry said, glancing at his watch.

We exited the island haven reluctantly but cheered up when we saw our guide standing on the porch and our fellow tourists lining up. After a brief introduction, our guide led us into the foyer.

"The entrance foyer contains some of the finest examples of faux-bois and open-pierced freize work in existence today," she said, gesturing to each. "The French chandelier is Baccarat crystal and weighs more than three hundred pounds. Take a look at the stained-glass entrance, which is original to the house. It was hand-painted, etched, and patterned after the French cross to ward off evil."

Harry and I gazed about in fascination as the guide continued. "There is a story that says this mirror," she said, gesturing toward it, "houses the spirits of Sarah Woodruff and two of her children, who were poisoned by a slave named Chloe."

The tour guide told us the legend of Chloe while beside me Harry snorted softly in derision.

"Mirrors were usually covered after a death," the guide went on, "but this particular mirror was overlooked. At one time or another, visitors have reported seeing ghostly handprints on the glass. You can see there are some strange drip marks running the length of the mirror. No one can remove them, no matter how frequently they clean this mirror."

A tourist beside me snapped a photograph of the drip marks.

"Visitors have also spotted figures in old-fashioned clothing lurking inside the mirror's warped glass," the guide concluded.

Then she told us more of the house's history. In 1834, the plantation was purchased by Ruffin Grey Stirling. The family remodeled the house, adding the broad central hallway in which we now stood and the entire southern section. The walls of the original house were removed and repositioned to create four large rooms including two parlors, a formal dining room, and a game room. The completed project nearby doubled the size of Whiskey Dave's house, and the name of the plantation was officially changed to the Myrtles around this time. Four years after the completion of the project, Stirling died of consumption. He left his vast holdings in the care of his wife, Mary Cobb, who managed to run all of the holdings almost single-handedly for many years.

Harry soaked in the lecture eagerly, glad we'd left the realm of the ghostly for the more pragmatic history. His enthusiasm was short-lived. The guide went on to recite the tragic story of Mary Cobb's son-in-law, William Drew Winter. According to the local paper, Winter was teaching a Sunday school lesson in the gentlemen's parlor in January of 1871, when he heard someone approach the house on horseback. A stranger called out that he had some business with him, so Winter went to meet him on the side gallery of the house. The stranger shot William and rode away, never to be seen again. Realizing that he was dying, Winter staggered inside the house and climbed the steps, trying to reach his beloved wife on the second floor. He died in her arms on the seventeenth step. Winter was buried the following day at Grace Church. His killer was never found.

"Both visitors and hotel employees have heard Winter's dying footsteps climbing the steps," the guide said, pointing to the staircase beside us.

The tour took us through the entire downstairs of the house. We saw the ladies' parlor (where a ghostly woman hums "Amazing Grace" and steals earrings), the dining room, the men's parlor, and finally the game room.

Harry lagged behind me as the tour entered the final room. I walked to the window to look outside as the other tourists clustered around our lecturing guide. I was hoping to see Chloe's phantom walking the grounds, but everything outside looked normal to me.

It was very cold beside the window, surprisingly so for summertime. I wondered if I was standing underneath an open vent, but none was apparent when I looked around. Where was the draft coming from? Then something bumped the bottom of my purse, one, two, three times, and I felt a yank on my skirt. I gazed down, annoyed that one of my fellow-tourists had invaded my personal space. There was no one there. I was standing alone by the window.

Good heavens.

I shivered in the cold spot surrounding me, spooked by my misbehaving handbag and the tug on my skirt. In the center of the room, the tour guide said: "Gaming rooms offered a restful and intimate atmosphere for games of chance. According to legend, the ghostly Woodruff children particularly like to haunt the dining room and the gaming room."

In the empty space beside me, someone—no, two someones—giggled. I felt another yank on my skirt. Then I heard a double pair of footsteps scamper away as Harry strolled up beside me and put his arm across my shoulders.

"You're shivering, honey," he said in concern. "We'll get your sweater from the car as soon as the tour is done."

I gazed up at my husband, wide-eyed with shock. Just behind Harry, two little voices were whispering together in the doorway. More giggles erupted, perhaps due to my pop-eyed look of disbelief. Then warm air flowed around us as the guide opened the exterior door to indicate that this was the end of the tour.

"Come on, honey," Harry said in concern. "I think you need some dinner."

My husband chivvied me gently outside and thanked the tour guide for both of us. I glanced back at the house as we moved away. For a moment I saw a small face pressed up against the window of the gaming room. The child smiled at me, then she pressed her hand over giggling lips and vanished.

"Harry," I said faintly, "I think I need a drink."

"Coming right up," my oblivious husband said and escorted me to the Carriage House Restaurant for a fine dinner and a very stiff drink.

7

Ghost on the Rooftop

ROYAL STREET, NEW ORLEANS

Life would be easier if Julie didn't love him quite so much, the young man thought moodily, swirling the whisky at the bottom of his glass. He'd met Julie at a masked ball and was struck by her beauty, culture, and wit. Julie was the sweetest girl he'd ever known. It had been easy to topple into love with her. Furthermore, he thought he'd be safe from womanly machinations with Julie. She had grown up in New Orleans society and she clearly understood that marriage was not an option between a woman of mixed heritage and a Creole gentleman. Such a thing was unheard of in the 1850s, as modern as the times seemed in other ways. If a Creole man married a woman of mixed heritage, his family would disinherit him. The Creoles zealously guarded their bloodlines, and any infraction was not tolerated.

Julie knew all this, the young man fumed into his cup. When he met her, she had calmly acknowledged her place within New Orleans society and was delighted when he suggested that they set up a fine apartment for her on the third floor of a house on Royal Street. But now, the sweetest girl he'd ever met had transformed into a shrew. Every night they spent together, she brought up the topic of marriage. "You are single. I am single," she said. "You come from a respectable family. I come from a respectable family. Why shouldn't we marry?"

Ha! As if his family would allow it. He lived comfortably now on the allowance they gave him. But the money would vanish if he wed Julie. And then what would happen to the pretty house on Royal Street, the easy life they now lived? The young man didn't think Julie would like working for a living any more than he, but that is what it would come to if they wed.

"Your family will not disinherit you," Julie scoffed. "They love you too much. You are worried about nothing."

The young man truly loved his Julie, and so he'd quietly sounded out his father on the matter. The tongue-lashing he received still made his cheeks turn pale with humiliation, many weeks later. He described the scene to Julie, hoping it would end her entreaties.

"Nonsense," Julie replied. "Your mother will talk him around."

"Even if she did, my whole family would be ostracized from New Orleans society. I will not be the cause of their undoing," the young man said.

By now the situation was so uncomfortable that the young man was forced to contemplate breaking things off entirely with Julie. He loved her deeply, but he could not live with her incessant demands. After Christmas, he would call it quits with Julie. He would leave her with enough money so that she could keep the apartment until she found another source of income. Until then, he would enjoy the company of the beautiful woman he loved and turn a deaf ear to her scolding. Decision made, the young man finished his drink, put on his hat, and headed for the apartment on Royal Street.

Julie was waiting for him, looking so lovely and sweet that the young man felt uneasy about his decision to leave her. She said nothing all evening about marriage. Their time together was so easy and free and romantic that it reminded the young man of the idyllic months when they first fell in love. It was only late that night when they were ready to sleep that Julie started crying, large tears rolling down her lovely cheeks. Once again, she begged the young man to marry her. He was equal parts annoyed by her demand and brokenhearted by her wretchedness. If he could convince her that marriage between them was impossible, they could still remain together. But how? He was struck with a sudden idea.

"All right, then, my darling Julie, I offer you a challenge. If you spend this cold December night naked upon this roof before the eyes of the whole town, I will marry you," the young man exclaimed, knowing his proud beauty would scorn such a challenge.

Julie was scandalized by the proposition, as he knew she would be. "What kind of woman do you think I am?" she exclaimed several times in a huff.

"No challenge, no marriage," the young man said and settled himself to sleep in triumph at having successfully countered Julie's irrational demands. Now he wouldn't have to break things off after Christmas, he thought happily as he drifted to sleep.

When he woke in the morning, Julie was no longer by his side. This was unusual behavior. He called her name, but there was no answer. The young man rose and searched the apartment for his love, wondering where she'd gone. Then he spotted something white lying on the floor near the door to the attic. It was Julie's nightdress. The young man remembered his challenge to Julie the previous evening, and his eyes widened. Surely she was not so desperate for marriage that she'd taken up his challenge. Was she?

With a curse, he charged up the attic steps two at a time and climbed out on the roof. He saw her at once, lying naked and still in the frosty morning, high above Royal Street where traffic was already stirring. She had frozen to death.

"Julie," he moaned, gathering up her still form. "Oh, Julie."

In that moment the young man saw at last into his own heart and bitterly regretted his words. They could have married in secret. They could have made it work. Maybe not in New Orleans. But somewhere.

The young man carried Julie downstairs and laid her tenderly on the bed. He would have her buried quietly someplace respectable and lovely, as befitted his sweet girl. It would need to be done discreetly, so the story did not come out and shame his family. But he would do right by his lovely lady this one final time.

A year passed. Once again, the young man was sitting by his fire in December, contemplating the charms of a woman. But this girl was much different than Julie. She was a Creole woman from a noble lineage, and the young man was courting her with a serious eye toward marriage.

The young man's thoughts were disrupted when a friend dropped by unexpectedly for a visit. "I suppose you've heard about the ghost," the friend said after they had settled before the fire with their drinks. The friend's words were spoken in an idle tone, but he watched the young man closely.

The young man was startled by the question. "A ghost?" he asked, wondering if his friend was drunk.

"There's a ghost over on Royal Street, in the house where you kept your octoroon before she died," the friend replied. "Several times this month, when the December nights grew cold, the ghost of a naked woman has been seen pacing up and down along the edge of the roof, trying to stay warm. Someone told me she looks like Julie."

The young man felt the blood recede from his cheeks. He took a long drink from his glass and set it down with shaking hands. "Exactly what are you implying?" he asked his friend.

"Nothing," the friend said. "I just thought you should know. In case word ever gets back to that Creole girl you are courting."

The young man paced agitatedly around the parlor for an hour after his friend left, wondering if the story of the ghost could possibly be true. Finally, the young man grabbed his coat and went down the once-familiar route to Royal Street. He settled himself near a lamppost on the opposite side of the road to watch the roof of the house where he'd found Julie's frozen body. An hour passed and then two as the air grew colder and traffic in the street died down. The young man was bored. This was silly. He was too sophisticated to believe in ghosts.

Then he saw her, standing naked and proud on the rooftop. She walked up and down, arms crossed before her chest, shivering in the cold. Sometimes she paused to thump life back into frozen limbs before resuming her walk. Finally, fatigued and cold, she sank slowly onto the roof and lay still.

The young man forced himself to watch the entire performance from beginning to bitter end; these were Julie's final moments, reenacted before his eyes on this cold December night. When Julie's body dropped to the roof, he broke down and wept for his lost love. And also for himself. With this ghost keeping the story alive, he would never persuade a girl from a good Creole family to marry him. He must leave New Orleans and live somewhere far away from the shadow of Julie and the third-floor apartment on Royal Street.

"I'm sorry, Julie," he whispered as the shadow of the octoroon woman vanished from the rooftop. "I'm sorry."

Clutching his coat tightly around his shivering body, the young man walked away and did not look back.

8

The Sausage Factory

NEW ORLEANS

My wife and I were introduced to Herr Mueller shortly after we moved to New Orleans. We quickly discovered that our families both hailed from the Black Forest region of Germany. In fact, we knew many of the same places and even had a few friends in common back in the old country. Eager to become better acquainted, Herr Mueller invited us to dinner in his home, and we were quick to accept his offer.

We met Mueller's wife over a meal of bratwurst and sauerkraut. Frau Miller was a sour-faced, bitter woman who—though only thirty-five—was wrinkled and old before her time. During the course of our dinner conversation, we learned that the couple owned a small sausage factory and that Frau Mueller's hard work had contributed not a little to their bottom-line income. Some people might think that Mueller was lucky to have such an industrious wife. Myself, I preferred my soft-spoken, pretty spouse and didn't care a whit how much she contributed to our bottom line. But each to his own.

A few months after we met the Muellers, the office in which I was employed as a bookkeeper burned to the ground. Herr Mueller generously offered me a job working in the office at the sausage factory. During the course of my new employment, I was able to witness up close the relationship between Herr Mueller and his Frau. It did not impress me. Frau Mueller was sharp-tongued and as hard as nails. Not an easy woman to live with. Or to work for, as I quickly discovered.

During my first month at the factory, Frau Mueller inspected my account books each night, down to the last penny. It was most disconcerting. She soon realized that I was an honest and ethical man who had no desire to cheat my employers. After the first month she left the bulk of the bookkeeping to me, merely inspecting the records once a week on payday. I took this as a high compliment from Frau Mueller. I could tell she liked me because she never complained of my work, and once she even gave me a compliment on my timeliness and the neat appearance of my office.

Frau Mueller was not so pleasant with the rest of the staff, and her treatment of Herr Mueller made my skin crawl. *Gott im Himmel* (God in Heaven), the woman never ceased complaining about her husband. And yet he bore the worst of her tongue-lashings with a smile on his face, as if he were deaf to her words. I could never understand it.

It was my wife who found out the truth. The greengrocer told my wife that Herr Mueller slipped out of his house each evening after Frau Mueller went to bed, to visit his plump girlfriend who lived a few doors down from the sausage factory. It was shocking behavior for a man who regularly went to church each Sunday. But it did explain how he could face his wife's bitter complaining with a smile on his face. Herr Mueller was cuckolding her. Frau Mueller did all the hard work at the factory and her husband used the hard-earned profits to shower his girlfriend with treats and take her to dinner.

Before I could decide what to do with this information, Herr Mueller came into the office to tell me his Frau had gone back East to visit her ailing mother. Mueller's cheeks were flushed, and he spoke rapidly, as if the news about his wife excited him. He was so chipper and jittery that morning that it made me nervous. Something didn't seem quite right to me. Perhaps he intended to divorce his wife while she was away? That would explain his nervous behavior. The negative press surrounding such a scandal would be dreadful, but Herr Mueller might think it worth the price of a lost reputation and customers to be rid of his Frau's complaints.

Mueller generously passed out bags of sausages to all his workers at the end of the day shift, something he would never have done if Frau Mueller were present. I took my heavy bag home and handed it to my lovely wife with a kiss. Dinner was already cooked, so she put the sausages in the cooler for another day. Over our meal, I told her about Frau Mueller's ailing mother and about Herr Mueller's strange behavior. "You may be right about the divorce," she said as she went to fetch a pot of coffee and dessert. "Poor Frau Mueller."

Throughout the following week, several of the factory workers dropped by my office to complain about Mueller's free sausages. "It was a terrible batch," the floor manager said one morning during his break. "No wonder Herr Mueller was giving them away. Did you eat any?"

"Not yet. To be honest, we put them in the cooler and forgot about them. My wife said she'd fry them up this evening for dinner," I replied.

"Tell her not to bother," the floor manager said. "The ones we ate had bits of bone in them and my daughter found blue threads in her sausage!"

My hand froze over the ledger, and I slowly set down my pen. The floor manager's daughter had found blue cloth in the sausages? That wasn't possible. Unless . . .

My body started trembling as suspicion blossomed in my mind. Frau Mueller wore a blue outfit to work every day. It was her favorite color. Oh, surely not. Surely Herr Mueller would never harm his own wife. It was a ridiculous notion. My thoughts were churning so hard that I barely heard the floor manager bid me a good morning as he returned to his duties.

I had a hard time acting normal when Herr Mueller popped into the office to discuss a few business particulars and assign me some extra duties. It was three days since his wife had left for the East Coast, and he was still acting jittery. His color was unnaturally high; his hands trembled when he gestured; and his voice was a touch too loud. Gott im Himmel, he was acting guilty. As if . . .

The extra work kept me busy until late that evening. There was almost no one left on the floor but Herr Mueller and myself when I finally finished my tasks. I was preparing to leave when I heard a "Thump! Thump! Thump!" sound coming from the main boiler vat. Alarmed by the noise, I rushed out onto the floor.

Herr Mueller was standing in the center of the room staring fixedly at the boiler, face snow-white and his body shaking. I followed his gaze and saw a greenish light approaching from the far side of the vat. The next moment, the glowing translucent figure of Frau Mueller appeared before us. Her head was crushed to a pulp and lolled obscenely against her left shoulder. Her body was misshapen and bloody. She looked as if she had been ground to pieces and then stuffed into a human-size sausage skin. One of her eyes had popped out of its socket, and the other rolled back into her crushed skull. Her mouth was lopsided; one side leered upward while the other twisted down. Her teeth were sharp splinters that cut grotesquely through the flesh of her lips. "Mueller," she moaned. "Come with me, Mueller."

I doubled over and vomited on the floor as the apparition stretched forth skinless, broken hands and grabbed the lapels of Mueller's coat. With surprising strength for such a misshapen corpse, Frau Mueller dragged her husband toward the sausage grinder. Mueller screamed in terror and beat at the phantom with both fists until she released him. Then he rushed out of the back door into the alleyway, still screaming. When Herr Mueller vanished, so did his dead spouse.

I wiped my mouth with a trembling hand and staggered out the front door, wanting to get away from Mueller and his ghost wife as fast as my legs would carry me. I was going to have to call the police, but what could I say to them? I couldn't tell them that I'd seen the ghost of Frau Mueller haunting the sausage factory. They'd lock me up!

I tottered home on legs that would barely hold me, wondering what to tell my wife. How could I ask her to believe in a ghost when I barely believed in it myself? When I reached the house, I found a police sergeant in the kitchen with my wife, who was having hysterics. The room stank of vomit, grease, and fried sausages. As soon as she saw me, my wife flung herself weeping into my arms.

"What is going on?" I asked the sergeant, who was scraping the remains of my wife's dinner into a bag.

"I cooked up those sausages you brought home from the factory," my wife sobbed into my shoulder. "The first sausage tasted fine, but I almost cracked a tooth on something hard inside the second sausage. There was a wedding ring buried inside the sausage," my wife gasped. "I recognized it at once. It belonged to Frau Mueller. The police think Herr Mueller murdered her by pushing her into the sausage grinder. And I just *ate* one of those sausages!"

She tried to vomit again, but there was nothing left in her stomach. I held her during the dry heaves and then cradled her gently against my chest. I knew exactly how she felt.

"We've sent some men around to arrest Herr Mueller," the sergeant told me. "I'm sorry, ma'am, but you will probably have to testify in court."

My wife nodded weakly, clutching me tighter.

"I've got her statement right here," the sergeant told me. "You look after your missus, now. She's had a bad day, but she did her duty like a trooper. Credit where it's due." He nodded politely to us both and exited with his bag full of evidence.

We learned later that the police found Herr Mueller in the alley behind the factory, rolled into a ball and screaming like a maniac. He said he'd seen his wife's ghost rise out of the meat grinder. "She's trying to pull me inside the grinder, too. She wants to make me into sausage," he sobbed. "But I won't go." He ended up in an asylum for the mentally insane.

A wealthy man purchased the factory after Mueller was committed, and tried to continue the profitable sausage business. But the ghost of Frau Mueller made so many gruesome appearances on the factory floor that the owner couldn't keep any worker longer than a week, and he was forced to close the shop forever.

As for me, I quit my job at the factory and found another position in a banking firm. And my wife and I never ate sausages again.

9

Madame's Revenge

As suicides went, it was fairly painless. Madame just put a gun to her head and pulled the trigger. That should have put an end to her misery. Sadly, things did not turn out as she had planned.

Madame stood looking down on her bloodstained body slumped on the floor, wondering what had gone wrong. Shouldn't she be in heaven (or the other place) right now? At the very least, she should have been snuffed from this existence! It hardly seemed fair that here she stood, still alone and miserable. And a ghost.

Of course, it was all the fault of that young man. Men were so selfish. Just because Madame was middle-aged didn't mean that she didn't deserve love and respect. After all, she was once a member of the chorus at the French Opera House and later became the owner of a successful pastry shop just around the corner from the opera.

A few years after she opened her pastry shop, which made a mint serving patrons of the opera, Madame hired a comely young man to work as her pastry chef. He had lied about his proficiency in the kitchen, but she taught him everything she knew and in the process toppled into love with him. There was such a disparity in their ages that she did not speak of her feelings. But when he began wooing her of his own accord, speaking eloquently of flowers and romance and moonlight walks along the banks of the Mississippi River, Madame could no longer resist her feelings. Soon, he was ruling the shop by day and her heart by night. She'd been so very happy that she hardly noticed when he wrangled a pay raise from her, and shorter working hours, and even carte blanche to charge whatever he wanted to her account. She should have known things were not as they seemed.

After six months of bliss, the other shoe dropped. The young man started murmuring the name Lisette in his sleep. Items of women's apparel appeared on Madame's monthly charge account, and none of them were gifts given to her. At last she had to face the truth. Not only was her lover making up to her to get special perks and extra income from his job at the pastry shop, but he was also seeing someone else. And not just seeing the floozy; he was actually living with her in a rooming house on St. Ann Street. Yet still he showered Madame with compliments, flowers and candy while he laughed behind her back at her gullibility.

Madame was miserable. Her world—yes, even her successful business career—lost all meaning. She begged him to return to her, but he scorned her love. That's when she decided to take her own life. But she could not let him go unpunished for his crimes against her. So she wrote a suicide note to the police, blaming everything on her former lover and hinting that her ghost would return to see that justice was done. And then she shot herself.

And became a ghost. It was maddening. Madame found a desk chair and sat in a corner, staring at the slumped figure on the floor and awaiting further events. It was not long before her landlady found the body and rushed screaming from the room. Then the police came and found her note. The sergeant—whom she recognized as a boarder at the rooming house where her former lover lived—actually laughed over the note, not believing a word she'd written.

Shaken with a sudden uncontrollable fury, Madame leaped to her feet and rushed the sergeant, clawing at him until red marks appeared on his face. Both policemen ran screaming in fear from the house. It was in that moment that Madame realized two things: people could see her disembodied form and she still had an impact upon the physical world. Her red-hot rage gradually faded into grim satisfaction. Perhaps she would have her revenge after all.

Things went a little dim after the police left. Madame fell into a half-sleep and only awakened at dusk the next night. This strange hiatus did nothing to alter her plan. When she awoke, she found herself standing on the front steps of the French Opera House, just around the corner from the pastry shop and down the road from her former lover's rooming house. She descended the steps and stalked along the road until she reached the corner of St. Ann and Royal, where her lover lived with his floozy. Madame walked right through the wood and metal trimmings on the closed front door and stood in the hall glaring at several borders that were coming along the hall. The young men gasped, and one girl fainted when she saw Madame's ghost.

Madame glanced into the mirror opposite the door and beamed in grisly satisfaction. Her dyed black hair was still intact, but her eyes glowed a demonic red and her bony, ashen face was withered and desiccated. How delightful! Now to scare the life out of her former lover and his floozy. She mounted the stairs and shoved her non-corporeal body through the locked door. The room was empty. Her lover was not at home. Madame glared at the pleasant space, noting all the feminine fripperies that the floozy had installed. How very domestic. She threw them all over the floor, thrust the window open and tossed all the floozy's dresses onto the ground below. The room was a terrible mess by the time she'd finished her work. As she gazed around in satisfaction, the strange dimness descended upon Madame and she vanished.

When she awoke, it was the next night and she was back on the front steps of the French Opera House. Again Madame made her way to the house where her former lover lived. And again he was not present.

On the seventh night Madame found the young man asleep with his floozy in the comfortable bed that should, by rights, have been hers. Triumphant, Madame went into the tiny kitchen, turned on the small stove, and watched as her lover and his girlfriend died from asphyxiation. When her lover drew his final breath, she vanished into the strange dimness that had claimed her each night since her own death.

Madame thought her punishment would be over when her lover died. But the haunting did not end. Every night, like a broken record, she reappeared at the opera house, stalked down the front steps, and went to her lover's apartment at the rooming house, which was rapidly losing boarders because of her. She must be under some kind curse, Madame decided, that kept her tied to this same routine each night; month after month, year after year.

A full decade had passed in rage and utter misery, when one day Madame jolted awake at noontime instead of dusk. What? Where? She shook her head in a daze, staring at the busy street in front of the French Opera House.

Then Madame had a sudden vision of a young woman standing by the fireplace in the room her former lover shared with his floozy, holding a stained yellow letter in her hand. And the ghost of Madame finally understood what was keeping her in this realm. As clear as a bell, she remembered the letter she had written in her despair, begging her lover to return to her. She remembered their final interview in his apartment, when her lover read part of her pleading letter aloud while his new girlfriend Lisette laughed in scorn. She remembered the shame and agony she'd felt as she stumbled back to her own apartment and committed suicide.

Madame roared in fury and launched herself down the steps of the French Opera House, scattering screaming pedestrians as her flaming figure sailed right through them and down the street. She must retrieve that shameful letter. Then, and only then, would her spirit be free.

Madame soared straight up to the second floor of her former lover's rooming house, burst through the window, and flew through the bedroom and into the sitting room, just in time to see the woman tenant toss the letter into the fire.

"Nooooo," Madame screamed, red eyes blazing in horror. "Nooooo!"

She leaped into the fireplace, her translucent hands clawing desperately at the flaming letter. But she could not grip it. Madame sank down onto the hearth and watched in dismay as the letter slowly crumbled to ashes. It was gone.

To her surprise, when the last piece of the letter vanished, so did her pain. With a sigh of relief, Madame felt dimness claim her for the very last time.

10

The Pirate's Ghost

LAFITTE'S BLACKSMITH SHOP

My wife hit the shops early and she hit them hard on our last day in New Orleans. By lunchtime, I was done with shopping. My head ached, my feet hurt, and I don't even want to think about what was happening to my budget.

Abbie was still raring to go. I swear that woman could keep shopping until midnight. As a compromise, we decided I'd meander over to the Lafitte's Blacksmith Shop where I could indulge my love of history by having a drink at one of the most historic (or was it notorious) spots in the city, and she'd join me after she'd had another crack at the shops.

The pirate Jean LaFitte was one of my favorite historical characters. Talk about a man of mystery! The infamous pirate-turned-war-hero didn't even have a known birthplace or birthdate. He could have been born in France or Haiti. He was born somewhere between 1780 and 1785. Historians couldn't even figure out where or when the man died.

Some facts were plain enough. Jean Lafitte and his brother Pierre were smugglers and pirates who worked their nefarious trade in the Gulf of Mexico. In the early 1800s, Jean Lafitte opened a blacksmith shop in New Orleans, which was a front for his smuggling business. Later Jean and his brother ran a group of pirates out of Barataria Bay south of the city with the help of Captain Dominique You.

During the War of 1812 Lafitte loaned supplies and men to General Andrew Jackson to help defend New Orleans against the British; he himself guarded one of the approaches to the city while the battle raged at Chalmette. Lafitte and his smugglers received an official pardon for their help in the war. When the Lafittes left New Orleans, they moved to Galveston Island in Texas and became spies for the Spanish during the Mexican War of Independence. They also developed a pirate colony called Campeche.

Lafitte continued attacking merchant ships around Central American ports until he vanished from recorded history in the 1820s, after he escaped from prison in Puerto Principe, Cuba, in February, 1822. Legend credits him with dying in Texas, Mexico, at sea, and in Illinois. The man really got around!

Lafitte's Blacksmith Shop was smaller than I expected, considering all the history that went with it. It looked rather out of place among the fancy Spanish architecture surrounding it. With just four rooms, it was cozy and snug. I found a small table in a corner and settled in to relax, drink soda (I was driving the car home that evening), and people-watch.

I'd read somewhere that members of the Lafitte Historical Society sometimes dropped by the shop in costume, and I hoped I'd timed my visit to coincide with their presence. I was not disappointed. Swashbuckling and proud, "Pierre Lafitte" strolled through the crowd around 3:00 p.m., followed by "Captain Dominique You." They swaggered about in full pirate costume and stayed in character no matter the remark tendered to them by the watchers in the bar.

I was disappointed when they left the room where I sat nursing my soda, to speak with other customers. Then I saw a third man standing quietly by the fireplace. His pirate costume was subdued compared to the other men, but he had long flowing black hair and a full beard. His air of quiet strength and intelligence impressed me. Was this the character actor playing Jean Lafitte? When he saw me glance his way, the dark-haired man approached my little table. "Ho, monsieur, what sort of ale is that?" he gestured to my diet soda.

"I'm not drinking ale today," I explained, waving him to take the seat opposite me. "I have to drive the car home after dinner."

"*Moi*, I do not understand these carriages that move without horses. *Mais non*," the man sighed in a light baritone, settling into the chair with his mug. "The world has changed so much since my day."

He swallowed some ale and then set his drink on the table. "This blacksmith shop was always full of people and goods, both legal and—shall we say—almost legal? I suppose it is fitting that it is still full of people. But I miss the old times."

"What were they like, the old times?" I asked, curious to see how the actor would describe the life of Jean Lafitte.

"Smelly," Lafitte said and flashed me a charming smile. I couldn't help smiling back. "Horse manure everywhere. No one bothered much with bathing in my day. Heavy perfumes were used to hide stench. Stinking mud in the streets whenever it rained. The smell, I confess, I do not miss!"

"I can't blame you for that," I said, sipping the last of my soda.

The server bustled over and asked if I wanted a refill. I was surprised that he didn't ask the same of my companion, but maybe there was some rule about not drinking to excess during a performance.

"I do miss my woman," Lafitte continued, moving his mug restlessly from hand to hand. "She had a lovely face and an even lovelier personality. We never married, which I sometimes regret. But it wasn't done, in those days, for a Frenchman to marry a woman of mixed heritage. My mistress followed me to Galveston, you know. We had many happy years together. She added a touch of softness to my life, which I dearly needed among all those smugglers and privateers. They were a raucous bunch, but most were brave men. Or maybe they were just foolhardy." He flashed another grin as he reminisced.

"Historians argue about who was the real boss, you or Pierre," I remarked as the server set a glass of diet soda in front of me.

The server gave me a puzzled look. "Excuse me?" he said. "Did you want to speak with 'Pierre Lafitte'? I can call him back."

"Not necessary," I said. "I was just speculating."

The server shrugged and left the table. My companion settled deeper into his chair and said: "Pierre was the elder brother. He ran the business end of things. I took more of a hands-on approach and spent much of my time with our men in Barataria Bay."

"What about the War of 1812?" I asked after a short silence fell between us.

"Ah, the war. The British were a threat to my part of Louisiana, and so I told the governor when I wrote to him," Lafitte said. "I offered my men to him, ready to exert their utmost efforts in defense of this country. Stray sheep wishing to return to the fold."

"Not completely without guile," I said. "You asked for a pardon."

Lafitte laughed. "*Oui*, monsieur. Pierre was not the only businessman in the family!" He chuckled and held up his mug in a salute to me.

At that moment I heard my name and turned to see Abbie bearing down on me from the door. I smiled and waved then turned to my companion to explain who she was. But the chair opposite me was empty. My stomach lurched in surprise. I was sitting in a corner. There was no way in or out except past me. Where had the actor gone? Was there some secret passageway in the wall right here?

Abbie appeared by my side. "I thought you weren't going to drink," she said, dropping a kiss on my cheek and sitting down in the recently vacated chair.

"I didn't drink," I protested, wrenching my attention from the little mystery to look at my wife.

"That's what they all say. Then why are you sitting alone in this corner talking to yourself? The folks at the bar were staring at you in fascination when I walked in," Abbie said.

"I wasn't talking to myself," I retorted, stung by her words. "I was talking to . . ."

I paused, color draining from my face. *Had* it been an actor occupying Abbie's chair? The server never spoke to him; indeed had reacted very strangely when he heard me talking to Lafitte. It was almost as if the server couldn't see or hear my table companion. And of course the blacksmith shop did have the reputation of being haunted by the ghost of . . . the ghost of . . .

I awoke on the floor of the bar with a crowd around me and Abbie patting frantically at my face. "Wh–what happened?" I asked groggily as Abbie told the bartender we didn't need an ambulance.

"You passed out," Abbie said. "At first I thought you were drunk, but the server said you only ordered diet soda. I think it's too hot in here. Would someone please help me get him outside and bring me the bill?"

The bartender lifted me up and helped me stagger outside. I sat on a nearby bench and breathed deeply of the fresh air. The world went a little gray when I remembered the remark Lafitte's ghost had made about the smell of this same New Orleans air back in his day. The bartender hovered beside me until Abbie came outside and took charge. Thankfully, it wasn't a far walk to the place where we'd parked. By the time we reached the car, I felt steady again, but Abbie insisted on driving us home.

Before she started the car, I told Abbie about my ghostly encounter. I didn't think it was safe to give her a supernatural explanation while she was driving. Abbie stared at me wide-eyed for a long time.

"I've got goose bumps all over my body," she whispered finally. "When I entered the bar, you were sitting alone at the table in the corner and it looked like you were talking to yourself."

"I wish I had been. It would be easier to believe," I said, slumping down into the passenger seat.

"But think how cool it is, honey, that you actually got to meet Jean Lafitte," Abbie said, her eyes sparkling suddenly. "Wow. That's just . . . wow!"

I smiled. Abbie could see the bright side in everything, even an encounter with a ghost. It's one of the reasons I'd married her.

"Yeah," I said and flashed my best "Jean Lafitte" grin. "Wow!"

We both laughed, and then Abbie turned the key in the ignition and drove us home.

11

Un, Deux, Trois

Oh, *mon Dieu*, but that old man was a miser! He lived in a wretched little cabin down by the Bayou Segnette, even though he had enough money to afford a mansion. He kept his wife dressed in rags and forced her to do all the work on the farm, while he wandered around all day gossiping about his neighbors and criticizing his wife.

The miser kept more than a thousand gold pieces buried under a loose floorboard. At night he would sit counting the coins after his wife fell into bed from sheer exhaustion. "*Un, deux, trois . . .*" he murmured, caressing the smooth gold coins and watching them gleam in the flickering lamplight.

The miser and his wife had one daughter, a sweet, cheerful girl who was very popular among the people of the Bayou. Everyone thought it was a shame the way her father kept her home from school and dressed her in rags while he himself wore fancy duds and swanked around town.

The daughter started working the farm as soon as she could walk, and never knew a day's rest. When her *maman* died, all the tasks for house and farm fell on the daughter, for her father refused to hire any outside help. The poor maiden tended the animals, planted the crops, cooked the meals, did the wash, and scrubbed the floors all by herself, while the miser sat inside the house counting his gold coins: "Un, deux, trois . . ."

One summer, yellow fever swept across the Bayou and the daughter fell ill. The miser was angry because she lay in the corner moaning and sweating instead of doing her work. He was forced to leave his lovely gold coins in the box and tend to the farm himself.

As the fever grew worse, the daughter begged her father to send for a doctor. "Doctors are expensive," the miser said, revolted by the very notion. "You don't need a doctor. You're just pretending to be sick to get out of work!" He slammed out of the house in a rage and went to the neighbor's farm to complain about his good-for-nothing daughter. When he returned to the house that evening, his daughter lay dead in her bed.

The miser was too stingy to give his daughter a funeral or bury her properly in an aboveground vault, as was the custom in the Bayou, where bodies buried in the ground would be swept from the grave during a flood. Instead, he tossed the dead body unceremoniously into a crude wooden coffin and buried her underneath a cypress tree near the river, with no gravestone or cross to mark the place where she lay.

The neighbors were scandalized by this lack of respect for his only daughter. "Mark my words, he will come to a bad end," they said to one another. "*Le bon Dieu* will see that justice is done."

But the old miser ignored the gossip and reluctantly hired a workman to help on the farm. He paid the man a tiny pittance and treated him so poorly that the hired man quit within a week.

No one else applied for the job, so the farm lay neglected while the old miser sat alone in the house day after day, counting his gold coins in the flickering lantern light: "Un, deux, trois . . ."

A month after the daughter's death, a huge hurricane rolled in from the Gulf. High winds lashed the trees. Rain fell in heavy sheets. The water in the Mississippi rose higher and higher, until it overflowed the levee. All the underground debris and buried things rose with the water level, including the cheap coffin buried under the cypress tree.

Inside the little cabin, the miser ignored the storm. He was counting his gold by the light of the lantern: "Un, deux, trois . . ." As the wind shook the walls and rain thundered on the roof, he held each coin up to the light, exulting in its round smoothness and the gleam of light across the gold surface.

All at once, something knocked on the front door: *Thud, thud, thud.* The sound reverberated through the small cabin. The miser jumped in surprise. "Who is there?" he shouted, annoyed that anyone would interrupt his solitary reverie. No one answered. "It must be a loose shutter," the miser muttered to himself, turning his attention back to his gold.

As he picked up the next coin, a cold wind blew around the room, ruffling the miser's white hair and making the wick of the lantern flicker wildly. The breeze sounded like a woman's sigh. "Faaaaaather. . . ." The miser ignored the wind.

The knock came again: *Thud. Thud. Thud.*

"Who's there?" shouted the miser.

A low moan echoed through the room, growing louder and louder. "Faaaaather. . . ."

The sound gave the miser goose bumps. He leaped to his feet and ran to the front window. No one was standing on the tiny porch. He glared around the cabin, but the little house was eerily silent. Even the howl of the wind and the lash of the rain were muted in the supernatural hush.

"It must be the neighbor's hound dog banging against the wall," the miser grumbled, trying to ignore the cold air pressing into his nostrils and turning each spoken word into a puff of frost. He sat down grimly and began counting again: "Un, deux, trois . . ."

Bang! Bang! Bang! The front door shook from the force of the blows. A woman's voice rose to a howl of anguish that shook the room from ceiling to floor: "Father! Send for the doctor. Father, help meeeeeeeeee!" The miser leaped to his feet, clutching the box of shiny gold coins to his chest.

"Un! Deux! Trois!" The woman's voice shrieked the numbers aloud. With each number the front door buckled under a tremendous blow. Then a cheap wooden coffin burst through the shattered remains of the portal, swept inside the cabin on a massive wave of floodwater. The coffin lid sprang back and a familiar decaying figure sat up and stretched rotting hands toward the miser. "Faaaaaaaaaather," the corpse hissed. The miser screamed.

When the flood waters receded, the neighbors went to check on the old miser. They found the small cabin filled with mud and debris. The old man himself was lying stiff as a board beside his chair, face twisted and dead eyes bulging with horror. Beside him, sitting upright in the open coffin, were the putrid remains of his dead daughter. A smile of triumph split her withered lips. In her rotting hands she clutched a wooden box filled with a thousand gold coins.

12

The Last Laugh

LAFAYETTE

Mes amis, it was well known throughout this parish that Thibodaux was a practical joker. *Mais oui,* he was the worst! He always wanted the last laugh, and he'd do just about anything to get it.

When Thibodaux was asked to watch over the house of a neighbor who was away on business, he moved all the bedroom furniture downstairs and put the kitchen table and the parlor set upstairs in the bedrooms. On Fat Tuesday, Thibodaux got up before dawn and rearranged all the street signs within ten blocks of the Mardi Gras parade so the out-of-town visitors got lost while he sat in the front row collecting beads and other treasures.

One summer Thibodaux made over $100 selling packets of donut seeds to the neighborhood children, guaranteed to grow the very best donut trees in New Orleans. Thibodaux was nearly run out of town when the parents found out about the prank. He had to apologize to the whole parish at the next town meeting, and he returned twice the value of the money he'd taken from the poor kids.

Thibodaux quit his joking for a while after the donut fiasco, but everyone knew he'd break out again sometime. He couldn't resist a practical joke.

Now Thibodaux's favorite target was his friend Boudreaux the shoemaker; a gullible fellow who took everything literally. *Pauvre* Boudreaux routinely poured sugar out of his salt cellar and drank the most vile concoctions known to man whenever he foolishly accepted a glass from the hand of Thibodaux. One evening a few months after the donut fiasco, Thibodaux and his friend went to the inn to have a drink. After a few pints of ale, Thibodaux said to his friend: "Boudreaux, *mon ami*, I bet you fifty dollars that you can't sit up all night with a dead body. You'd be running for the door before midnight!"

"I'm not scared of a corpse," Boudreaux protested. "I could sit up all night with a thousand dead bodies and never turn a hair!"

"Prove it, then!" Thibodaux said. "There's a corpse down at the church tonight, ready to be buried in the morning. If you sit up with it all night, I'll give you a hundred dollars. But if you run away before dawn, you'll owe me a hundred."

"I'll do it," said the thrifty shoemaker. The men shook hands on the bet and Boudreaux set off at once, staggering somewhat hazily down the road toward the church and his gruesome task. He swung by his house on impulse to pick up his shoemaking tools and a lantern. Since he was going to sit up all night, he might as well get some work done.

Thibodaux, of course, had long planned this practical joke. He'd made a wooden coffin and placed it inside the church. And the knapsack he carried to the inn contained a dead man's shroud to wear and some charcoal to smudge under his eyes to make himself look hollow-faced and lifeless. As soon as Boudreaux left the bar, Thibodaux raced ahead to the church to put on his costume and lay down in the coffin. "Boudreaux won't be able to resist peeking inside, and then I'll grab him.

He'll be so scared he'll run squawking like a frightened hen. This is the easiest hundred dollars I've ever made," Thibodaux chuckled.

Just then he heard footsteps coming into the sanctuary. Thibodaux held his breath and watched through a crack in the lid as Boudreaux peered cautiously around the candlelit room.

"Any minute now he's going to come over and look inside," Thibodaux whispered gleefully.

Then he heard Boudreaux say: "I ain't going to look in that coffin. You've seen one corpse, you've seen them all. I'll just pull me up a chair and get some work done on these custom-order shoes."

So Boudreaux sat on a hard-backed chair beside the coffin and started tacking the heels onto a new pair of shoes with his hammer: *A-rat-a-tat, a-rat-a-tat.*

Thibodaux waited and waited for his friend to peek inside the coffin. But Boudreaux was too literal-minded to be bothered by a corpse, and he stuck to his task. *A-rat-a-tat, a-rat-a-tat* went the hammer on the shoe heel as Boudreaux beat in the nails, one by one.

"I'd better do something quick, or Boudreaux will win the bet," Thibodaux muttered.

He thought awhile and then decided to make some noise of his own. So Thibodaux knocked on the side of the coffin: *Tap-tap-tap. Tap-tap-tap.* The noise sounded so much like the rapping of the hammer that Boudreaux never looked up from his work.

Thibodaux was feeling restless and uneasy in his cramped resting place. He hadn't expected to spend the night in a coffin, and he didn't like the idea one bit. So he knocked harder: *Tap-*

tap-tap. Tap-tap-tap. And glory be, the cobbler finally looked up from his work.

Boudreaux rose from the chair and went to the church door. He looked outside, but no one was there. "Must be a tree branch knocking against the side of the church," he said and sat back down to his work.

Thibodaux was feeling a mite claustrophobic inside the narrow coffin. He wanted out of that dad-blame box, even if it meant spoiling the joke. But he had to give it one last try. So Thibodaux pounded as hard as he could on the side of the coffin: *Bang-bang-bang. Bang-bang-bang.*

Boudreaux jerked upright and stared wide-eyed at the coffin. Finally . . . finally! He walked over to the pine box, hammer in hand, and slowly raised the lid. Thibodaux sat up at once, sweating in sheer relief, and moaned: "A man sitting with the dead shouldn't work!"

"Dead men shouldn't talk," Boudreaux retorted in a panic. He slammed his cobbler's hammer down on Thibodaux's head, killing him stone-dead. As the practical joker fell backward into the coffin, Boudreaux cried: "That'll teach you not to talk, dead man!"

Then Boudreaux took a second look at the corpse in the coffin and realized it was his friend Thibodaux. Boudreaux gasped and sank onto the chair, his whole body trembling in shock. Slowly, his too-literal mind pieced together the sequence. Thibodaux had played a practical joke on him, hoping to win a hundred dollars by scaring him into running away. And he—Boudreaux—had accidently killed his friend.

Boudreaux wondered what he should do. He didn't want to go to prison. Then he realized that the solution was right in front of him. Thibodaux was already shrouded and lying in his coffin. Thibodaux was ready to go if any man was. So Boudreaux dragged the coffin into the churchyard and dug a hole in the farthest corner among the old graves. When he was done digging, Boudreaux raised the lid one last time and bid his old pal good-bye. "I'm sorry, Thibodaux, that your joke backfired," Boudreaux said. "This time you didn't get the last laugh." He used his cobbler's hammer and nails to fix the lid in place and then pushed the coffin into the new grave.

As the box slid downward, Boudreaux felt something tighten around his neck. "Mais *non*," he cried in sudden panic, realizing he'd just nailed his tie to the lid of the coffin! "Thibodaux, let gooooo!"

Boudreaux grabbed for the edge of the box, trying to pull the coffin back up, but it was too heavy. The coffin slid inexorably down into the hole, cutting off Boudreaux's air supply and pulling him into the grave with his friend Thibodaux.

When the church sexton arrived for work the next morning, he found an open grave containing two bodies. Boudreaux lay draped over the coffin, strangled to death by his own tie. And Thibodaux lay prone inside the box, beaten to death by Boudreaux's hammer.

The parish erected a fancy tombstone over a double grave containing the practical joker and the cobbler. On one side of the tomb, the epithet said: "He who laughs last, laughs best." And on the other side, it read: "Dead men don't talk."

These days, whenever folks hear a rapping sound inside the old church, they say it is the ghost of Thibodaux trying to get the last laugh on his old friend. And whenever they hear a thump in the graveyard, it is Boudreaux the cobbler nailing his tie to the lid of Thibodaux's coffin.

13

The Specter's Treasure

Mentor Quigley was an inventor at heart, though he earned his living as a clerk at a drugstore. In the evenings while his wife Delia knitted by the fire, he worked with orange peel and vanilla beans and other foods, trying to create flavoring extracts that could save the local housewives much time and make him rich besides.

Late one afternoon on his way home from work, Mentor had one of those inspirational flashes that in past days have caused men to shout "Eureka" and leap about. As he thrashed out the details of his new idea, Mentor wandered far afield until he was walking in a shady part of town. He didn't hear the footsteps behind him until a moment before a blow struck him on the head.

Several hours later, Mentor awoke with a headache and empty pockets. As he sat numbly in the grass, he saw the bobbing light of a lantern approaching him down the shell road. An old man with sparkling blue eyes and a short white beard stopped when he saw the young clerk bleeding by the wayside.

"Let me help you up, young fellow. You been in a fight?" he asked, extending a hand to Mentor. The clerk took it gratefully and staggered to his feet.

"Robbed," he said briefly, fighting dizziness and nausea.

"Come along to my shack and rest a bit," the old man said. "Lean on me."

Gratefully, the young clerk did as instructed and the old man guided him down the shell road to his shack.

"What's your name, young fellow?" his old rescuer inquired, settling the young man down on the small cot.

"I'm Mentor Quigley," the clerk mumbled, lying back against the pillow with a sigh of relief.

The old man's face lit up. "You don't say! Son of Matthew Quigley, grandson of old Israel Quigley?"

The clerk's eyes popped open in surprise. "That's right. How do you know that?"

"Because I'm Israel's brother Adam," the old man said. "We were raised in Connecticut afore Israel moved south and I went to Californy after gold. I've just got settled here in town and I've been hoping to find my brother. Israel wrote and told me that he'd moved to New Orleans. How is he?"

Mentor, listening with astonishment to this explanation, frowned sadly and said: "Dead these fifteen years."

Adam Quigley shook his head sadly. "How about my nephew Matthew that I've never seen? Dead, too?"

"Father's still alive but dying of cancer on his face. He's not expected to live," Mentor said.

"Ach, lad, I am sorry," old Adam said. "I never expected to outlive the rest of my family. Save yourself, of course. So what about you, lad, you married?" he said, picking up the thread of their conversation where they'd left off.

"Very happily," Mentor said. "Delia and Father will be so glad to meet you, Great-Uncle Adam!"

And so they were. Delia scolded Mentor soundly for wandering off and then kissed the cheek of her newfound great-uncle Adam when she learned that he had rescued her erring husband. Matthew grinned weakly and challenged his uncle to a game of checkers.

The family wanted old Adam to move in with them, but he was an independent fellow, happy living in his shack with his old burro Nelly. Old Adam had done well in the goldfields of California. "I'm fair lined with gold. I keep it as close as my skin," old Adam often said with a wink. He never mentioned how much money he made in the goldfields or where he kept it, and the family didn't press him for details.

Uncle Adam was always leaving money inside the family Bible or tucked under the milk jug to help his relations make ends meet. Mentor always turned this money over to Delia, who knew how to stretch a penny to its utmost. One day old Adam took Mentor aside and said: "You're all I've got left once Matthew goes, my boy. I'm leaving my money to you and that pretty wife of yours. Meantime, I'm going to bury my gold to keep it away from robbers and such. I ain't told no one the location but the little black beetles and my burro Nelly, so the secret's safe enough. But when my time comes, I'll let you and Delia know where you can find it."

A few days later, Mentor read in the paper that an old man named Adam Quigley was murdered on the shell road along Baseline. According to the report, people around town thought old Adam was carrying his wealth on his person and it was thought that someone had lured him away from his shack to rob him of his treasure. Two local men found the old man's body with its throat cut from ear to ear. They reported the crime at once, but by the time the police arrived, the body had vanished. Carted away by the murderers, it was supposed. The spot where the murder took place was well known to the locals because the workmen had just finished repairing a bad hole in the road at that location. The police searched high and low for the old man. When they investigated his shack, they found the corpse of poor Nelly the burro. Her head was nearly severed from her little body. No money was found in the shack.

The Quigley family was devastated by the news. Mentor went to the police at once, but there was nothing further the officials could do in the case. As the old man's closest relative, Mentor went to the shack to claim his meager possessions and search for clues to Great-Uncle Adam's murder. Both he and Delia were sure that the murderers had stolen all of their great-uncle's money before he had time to bury it in the place "known to the beetles and old Nelly."

Mentor found nothing in the small building except his great-uncle's old felt hat and a jug of alcohol sitting on the floor by the cot. The sight of the jug brought Mentor to tears. Whenever he stopped by for a visit, his great-uncle would point to the jug and say: "It ain't to drink. That alcohol's for hardening purposes. It keeps your skin tough but flexible, like a leather saddle flap. You should try it! It makes a man irresistible to the ladies!" Old Adam would rub his leathery cheeks for emphasis, and Mentor would laugh and say: "That alcohol looks good on you, Great-Uncle."

"They got away with everything," Mentor told Delia that night. "Poor Great-Uncle Adam."

Shortly after old Adam's death, the Quigley family heard rumors of a new phantom that appeared suddenly on the old shell road at midnight. Terrified witnesses said the specter had a short white beard and a bloody throat slashed from ear to ear. The ghost appeared at the very spot where the two pedestrians said they'd found old Adam's murdered body.

Mentor was worried by the story of the ghost. Was it his great-uncle come back from the grave, or was it merely a some kids playing a practical joke? He wished he could discuss the matter with Delia, but his father had taken a turn for the worse and his good wife was run ragged caring for the cancer-ridden man.

When ghostly reports continued for more than a month, Mentor knew he had to investigate. Old Adam must have a reason for returning from the grave. Mentor brought the matter up with Delia one evening after supper, and she agreed to bring a neighbor in to care for Matthew while Delia took some well-deserved time off. "Don't expect us until very late," Delia told the neighbor. "It would be best if you sleep over in the dressing room and go home in the morning. We will sneak in quietly so we don't wake you or Matthew."

The Quigleys hired a buggy from the local livery stable and filled it with a picnic dinner and some not-so-usual items like a large square of sailcloth, a lantern, and a spade. Then they drove to old Adam's shack and waited inside until midnight, the time when rumor said the ghost was most likely to be seen on the shell road. Then they carried the lantern, sailcloth, and spade to the newly repaired place in the shell road where the specter walked, hiding in the bushes whenever a late carriage drove past.

"Do you think Great-Uncle Adam will come?" Delia whispered as they huddled together in the bushes just out of sight.

"I don't know," Mentor replied then placed a finger to his lips when he heard the rattle of an approaching carriage.

Suddenly the temperature on the road plummeted. Delia shivered and clutched her husband's arm as a white figure materialized right in front of the carriage horses, causing them to rear while the occupants of the carriage shrieked in terror. The specter shone with a bright inner light, weaving back and forth across the bump in the road. The leathery, white-bearded face of old Adam was clearly visible, his throat slashed from ear to ear, just as the two witnesses had described in the newspaper. Blood poured horrifically from the gaping wound, but it did not stain old Adam's clothing or his snow-white beard. The stench of rotting corpse wafted on the wind, driving the horses mad with fear. Then the specter melted into the bump in the road and the horses plunged forward, the carriage careening wildly from side to side as they raced away.

"That was Great-Uncle Adam," Delia said urgently into her husband's ear. "Mentor, I think the murderers buried him right here on the shell road!"

Once the road had been deserted for more than an hour, the couple went to examine the bump in the shells. "Look," Delia said suddenly, pointing to a moving black line of bugs. "Little black beetles. Mentor, didn't Great-Uncle Adam say something about telling the beetles where he buried his gold?"

"I'm going to dig up the bump," Mentor said decisively.

The road hadn't had time to settle properly in the newly repaired hole. The digging was absurdly easy. About two feet down, Mentor's spade struck metal. A moment later, he uncovered a steel box. It took some serious hoisting for the couple to lift the heavy object out of the hole. They smashed open the lock with a stone. The box was packed with gold coins, and the letter on top contained old Adam's will leaving all his money to Mentor and Delia. It was witnessed by six local men just a month before old Adam's death.

"Three of these men left town right after Great-Uncle Adam's murder," Mentor said grimly to his wife. "But they didn't get this box. He must have buried it right after he made the will, just after the road workers completed their work."

"The box may explain the presence of Great-Uncle Adam's ghost," Delia said thoughtfully. "But dig a little farther, Mentor, just to be sure. If Great-Uncle Adam is buried here, I want to dig him up and give him a proper burial, as befits a Quigley."

Mentor hid the box in the bushes by the road and kept digging. Less than a yard from the place where they unearthed the box, the spade hit a leather boot. Face grim, Mentor Quigley dug up the body of his beloved great-uncle Adam. Carefully he hoisted the corpse onto the sailcloth that Delia had spread out upon the shells.

"Both Great-Uncle Adam and the murderers took advantage of the newly mended road," she mused. "They never dreamed how close they were to his treasure."

"We must hurry back to the shack," Mentor said. "It is only a few hours until dawn."

Mentor quickly filled in the holes in the road while Delia wrapped the body in the sailcloth. Then he lifted his great-uncle's body carefully to his shoulder while Delia fetched the steel box. The corpse was extremely heavy for such a thin old man. Mentor staggered under the weight and had difficulty keeping up with his wife as she led them down the path to the old man's shack.

Once inside the relative safety of the shack, they discussed what to do next. The gold was theirs, no contest about that. But how would they explain the presence of their great-uncle's murdered body? The men who witnessed their great-uncle's will would surely accuse them of his murder should the circumstances become known.

Suddenly the wind rattled against the door of the shack. It sounded like someone knocking. A bit of paper blew under the gap at the bottom and landed by Mentor's foot. The couple stared at each other in surprise, and then Mentor picked up the paper. It was torn from the flyleaf of an old book. Most of the words had been washed away by water, but a single phrase stood out: "Look under the skin. . . ."

Mentor gulped suddenly, remembering the jug of alcohol his great-uncle used to keep his skin "flexible like a saddle flap." At the same moment, Delia's eyes widened and she whispered: "You said the body was heavy. . . ."

"Go out to the buggy, Delia," Mentor said grimly. "I am going to have a look."

Nearly an hour passed before he called his wife inside. Mentor was ashen-faced and trembling in the lantern light. "Great-Uncle Adam made pockets out of his skin and put a single gold coin in each pocket," he told Delia, rubbing his mouth in revulsion. "There were hundreds of them from his shoulders to his knees. Everywhere he could reach. He sewed up the slits, and the skin healed over the coins. I pulled out every last one of the coins and put them in the sack by the door. His body is very light now." He turned away on the last word, fighting to control his breathing. It had not been a pleasant task.

"We can't leave him here, Delia," Mentor said once his voice was back under control. "He's Great-Uncle Adam. What should we do?"

They heard a happy chuckle over by the corpse in the sailcloth. Delia stared aghast at the white light hovering there. Then she relaxed with a smile, and the white light vanished.

"That was Great-Uncle Adam," she said simply. "He said we should put him in my bonnet and the linen duster to make him look like me. If you get home before dawn, no one will ever know."

"But what about you? You cannot walk all the way back home," Mentor protested. "It's too far."

"I walk longer distances every day going about my chores," she replied with a smile. "Please, dearest. This is the only way."

And so Mentor placed his great-uncle's body beside him in the buggy and drove home in the twilight just before the dawn. He parked next to the side door of the house and whisked the light body upstairs to the attic without waking his father or his caretaker. He even had time to put the bag and box full of gold in the attic with his great-uncle and lock the door before he heard the neighbor stirring in the dressing room.

Mentor thanked the sleepy neighbor for watching over his father and asked the elderly woman to please excuse his wife from seeing her off, since Delia was feeling a bit under the weather. "A release from stress does that to some folks," the old lady said wisely. She promised to bring over some calves-foot jelly the next day and then toddled off, none the wiser.

Mentor sent a note to the drugstore, begging leave to stay home for the day, saying his father's condition was worse. He spent the morning tending his father and waiting for his wife to come home. Delia arrived at midday, dusty but safe and sound. She napped in Matthew's dressing room while Mentor took the buggy back to the livery stable. Then the two of them sat down and told Matthew what they'd found under the bump in the shell road.

Matthew died a week later and they laid him out in a closed casket, telling everyone that the cancer had disfigured his face. In reality, the body of Great-Uncle Adam lay in the casket beside his nephew. After the mourners left the house for the last time, a white shape materialized beside the casket, chuckling happily.

"Great-Uncle Adam is pleased," Delia said, smiling at the crackling white glow. The specter nodded to his relatives and vanished with a friendly popping sound.

"I think he likes fooling people," Mentor said. "He told people that he was 'fair lined with gold' and that he 'kept it as close as his skin.' And that was the exact truth!"

"We will put a memorial to Great-Uncle Adam on the back side of Father's tombstone. A two-for-one deal," Delia said.

"You can't ask fairer than that," Mentor replied.

PART TWO
Powers of Darkness and Light

14

Preemptive Strike

ST. LOUIS CEMETERY NUMBER THREE, NEW ORLEANS

It was our first visit to New Orleans and we were so excited that my nephew could barely sit still as we drove into the city and searched for parking. (Neither could his mother.) There were three of us visiting the city that day: Davey, his mom, and me, his aunt.

New Orleans is a city with a supernatural reputation and, thus, was of special interest to us, since a paranormal sixth sense runs through our paternal family line. My sister can see visions of the past and has seen ghosts more than a time or two. I am a healer with a reputation for calming paranormal sites and bringing tense situations back into balance when things go awry on the spiritual plane. It was too soon to know how Davey's talents would manifest, but he seemed to be following in his mom's footsteps.

Like many tourists, we gravitated toward the Steamboat and got tickets for the lunch cruise on the Mississippi River. With time to spare, we opted for a historical tour of the city first, with a ghost tour to take place the next evening.

We hopped on the bus, cameras poised, and Davey got first dibs on the window. The bus traveled along famous streets, past houses both historical and lovely. The history and folklore of New Orleans flowed eloquently from our tour guide, and we listened in fascination as he described the famous places and people who once lived in the city. Then the bus driver stopped at Cemetery Number Three so we could get out and walk among the tombs while he described the burial customs of old New Orleans.

We descended into midday heat, and Karen and I exchanged uneasy glances. I was completely on edge even before we walked through the gates. I wasn't sure I wanted to visit a New Orleans cemetery, but since it was broad daylight and there were a lot of people around, I figured it must be okay. Karen seemed drawn to certain grave markers and studied them closely, but I stayed in the middle of the grassy aisle, keeping away from the graves. Instead, I used the zoom lens on my camera to look at the detailed inscriptions and carvings.

Suddenly I was overcome with dizziness and staggered for a moment, off balance. I lowered the camera and shook my head, trying to clear it. What in the world? I rubbed my eyes and decided it must be the heat of the New Orleans summer getting to me. Our summers weren't so hot in New York.

Karen and Davey were ahead of me, following close to the guide. I straightened, took a deep breath, and staggered to catch up, not quite sure what had just happened. My enthusiasm for photography waned, and I longed for the cool of the bus. I was at the head of the line when we boarded, and Karen eyed me with concern as she sat down. "It is probably the heat," I told her, and we decided to purchase a bottle of water at our next stop.

I dozed off and on during the rest of the tour, feeling exhausted and grumpy. This was not how I had planned my first visit to New Orleans. The bottle of water helped somewhat, but I was still under the weather when we parted company with the bus tour and walked over to the Steamboat for the lunch cruise. I settled into the air-conditioned dining room and stayed there while Karen and Davey explored the ship.

I was still dragging after our late lunch, but I summoned enough strength to waltz with Davey on the ship's dance floor and watch the huge wheel at the back of the ship as it propelled us down the mighty river.

I was longing to leave the city and check into our hotel in the suburbs. Maybe I just needed to get a good night's rest. It took me awhile to chivvy the others off the boat and away from the fascinating crowds on the riverfront. Street performers were playing jazz and clowning around. One mime took a fancy to Davey and had the crowd in stitches as he set my nephew in a cool performer's pose walking an invisible dog.

But finally (finally!) we were in the car and driving out of New Orleans, followed by a humdinger of a thunderstorm. It was extremely annoying being in such close quarters with my sister and nephew. My grumpy mood was contagious, it seemed. The hotel arrived not a moment too soon. Check-in was one annoyance after another. A spectacular downpour started just as we arrived, making it impossible to bring in the luggage. The delay at the front desk was protracted, and then Davey lost the only key to the room he shared with his mother (how can you lose a key in a straight hallway less than one hundred yards from the front desk?). Waiting in my room for his mom to get a replacement, Davey jumped up and down on the bed as if he were possessed, jabbering away at a mile a minute as he raced around the small room. It was a bit hard to take.

As soon as Karen got back with the new key, I escaped into the downpour to move the car closer to our rooms and get the luggage. As I raced through the pouring rain, a massive stroke of lightning slammed into the ground about a hundred yards from me, electrifying the air and standing my hair on end. Good Lord, that was close! I jumped into the car for protection, heart thundering in sudden panic. What the heck was wrong?

I discovered too late that I had left the key in the room when I made my getaway from my suddenly manic nephew, so I had to go back to the front desk for another one and then run back and forth in the rain to haul luggage to two different rooms.

When I stopped at Karen's door, she informed me that my crazy nephew had just jumped into the shower fully clothed. Good grief. This was wild behavior from a kid who complained about getting wet in the rain.

Exhausted, I spent a few minutes alone in my room, trying to calm down and lighten my dark mood. It felt as if something was sapping all my strength (and with it my patience) right out of my system. Normally nothing Davey or Karen said or did disturbed my equilibrium. What was wrong with me? Had I gotten sunstroke in that cemetery? How long did sunstroke last, anyway?

Once Karen had hauled her errant son out of the shower and gotten him into dry clothes, we went to dinner across the street (that's as far as any of us wanted to travel!). Both Karen and I had gotten some bad vibes while we explored New Orleans, and Davey's wild reaction just now concerned us both. We decided to visit the zoo and do kid-friendly things the next day. We needed a break from supernatural New Orleans.

The food did not restore my energy. I felt as if I were walking wounded by bedtime. I barely managed to get into my jammies before I fell into bed. Literally. I was asleep as soon as my head touched the pillow.

I snapped awake at 1:00 a.m., sure that someone had spoken my name in the empty bedroom. I sat up, puzzled, and was instantly overwhelmed with a vision of myself, lying in the bed with a dark abomination attached to the center of my back. The creature was sucking the energy and strength and goodness out of my system. It was feeding on me. I knew at once that the vision was true. It was a warning, delivered to me from someone (my guardian angel?) on the inner planes.

With a flash of insight, I realized what had happened. This abomination, this tiny demon, had seen me in Cemetery Number Three, where it lived, and it had ambushed me. It was a preemptive strike against a spiritual healer who was not welcome by some of the dark powers that lived in this supernatural city. The creature had fooled me. I routinely guard against dark spiritual forces before I attend a ghost tour. But this attack had come on a sunny day while I was taking a history tour.

A tour that, my subconscious whispered, included a stop at a cemetery.

But it was bright daylight, I protested.

And then I realized that this, in and of itself, was a testament to how strong the dark creatures were in this city. And I also discerned that it was in the nature of this foul creature to camouflage itself as something else (like heat exhaustion). That was how it got past my defenses.

Suddenly I was furious. I glared at the creature with my spiritual eyesight. It cringed, knowing the jig was up. Knowing it could never pull this trick again; at least not on me. With just a few holy words and a prayer, I sent it reeling off my back. A few more words and it hurtled out of the hotel and then right out of this dimension. "DON'T COME BACK," I roared after it, brushing my hands together.

After doing some calming meditation, I rolled over and went back to sleep. As I drifted off, I thought: *Now I know why Davey was acting so crazy. It wired him up to be in an enclosed space with that creature.* And, of course, all our mishaps had started after we visited the cemetery.

The next morning I told Karen what had happened, and she nodded her head at once in confirmation. It tallied up with what she'd observed the previous day. We both decided that we needed to be on our guard that day and should probably not take any of the more serious ghost or voodoo tours. Instead, we scheduled a nice, kid-friendly ghost tour in the middle of the afternoon. Better to be safe than sorry, especially in New Orleans!

15

Shriveled Hearts

MISSISSIPPI RIVERFRONT, NEW ORLEANS

September 15, 1804. From the doorway overlooking the riverfront, a voodoo priestess stood watching the sailors load the last of the supplies into the hull of the slave ship and prepare for launch. Busy with their tasks, none of them saw a shadow slip up the gangplank and disappear into the hold. The priestess smiled grimly. This was one ship that would not return to New Orleans with its cargo of despair. As the sailors cast off from the dock, she turned her back on the scene and stalked away.

October 1, 1804. A knock on the door interrupted the captain in mid-sentence as he wrote in the ship's log. The captain's hand jerked and ink spilled over the page. The seaman cursed aloud before shouting gruffly: "Come in!"

The first mate loomed in the doorway, face pale, mouth set. "Sir, I was just informed that a third sailor has died of the wasting sickness. The doctor wishes to perform an autopsy on the bodies to see if anything can be done to spare the rest of the crew."

The captain swiveled in his chair. "An autopsy, you say? I don't hold with them. 'Tis against nature to cut up a body when it's already dead."

"But to save a life, sir?" the first mate prompted.

The captain frowned reluctantly. "Very well. Keep me informed."

The mate had the bodies lined up by the mainmast, and the ship's surgeon carefully performed the autopsies. He found the same thing in each case: The blood in each body was thick and sticky like treacle honey, and the heart of each man was shriveled and dried up like a hard kernel inside a peach. If they hadn't been in the correct part of the anatomy, the surgeon would never have taken them for hearts.

The captain, summoned from his cabin, glared at the bodies that were disturbing the peace of his journey. "What kind of disease shrivels hearts?" he demanded, staring at the four dried-up husks lying beside the bodies.

"I don't think it is a disease, Captain," the surgeon said, wiping his trembling hands on a handkerchief. "I've never seen nor heard of anything like this."

"It's a curse," whispered one of the watching sailors gathered behind the mast.

"Belay that!" snapped the captain. "I don't believe in curses. Get those blasted bodies off my ship. Now!"

He gestured toward the sea, and the sailors obediently threw the bodies over the side with no regard for a proper sea burial.

The surviving members of the crew were stricken with fear and loathing. They took to wearing lucky amulets and written prayers in their pockets, hoping to ward off the curse. But again and again sailors would awaken pale and trembling or would falter in the midst of the morning tasks. Within an hour of the first symptoms, they fell down dead and the captain had their bodies pitched overboard to feed the sharks.

October 15, 1804. They were less than a week out of Africa when the captain summoned the first mate to his cabin. "Why is this happening?" he roared. "We've lost more than half our crew. If this curse continues, we won't have enough men to sail back to New Orleans. Find out what's causing these deaths, man, or I swear I will throw *you* to the sharks."

The first mate swallowed hard. The captain meant every word. If he didn't discover the cause, he would die. Unless the curse caught up with him first.

"Aye, aye, Captain," he whispered through dried lips.

"Dismissed," the captain bellowed.

The first mate hurried from the dim room into the orange and gold of a beautiful sunset. He barely saw it. In his mind he could already see the sharks circling his thrashing body in the cold water. He could picture their mouths wide open, sharp teeth aimed at his throat.

The first mate lay awake long into the night, unable to shake the images in his mind. He didn't know what to do. If the mystery had baffled the ship's surgeon, the smartest man on board, how could he, an uneducated first mate, solve it? He wasn't normally a praying man, but that night the first mate prayed that God would show him the answer.

The first mate woke in the deep darkness before dawn when a hand shook his arm. The hand covered his mouth before he could speak. He opened his eyes wide, staring above him, but no one was there. At least, no one in the flesh. Some mysterious sixth sense made him turn his head to look through the small gap in the curtain around his hammock. A malevolent red light glowed faintly outside in the hold. In the savage light, he saw an old crone scuttle past his bunk, carrying a black candle that was the source of the evil glow. She bent over the bed of the second mate in the bunk across from his hammock and covered the man's chest with her ringed fingers.

The first mate's blood ran cold with fear and his skin prickled with sweat at the sight, but he was no coward. He tried to leap up and rescue his comrade from the evil crone, but the invisible presence kept him bound to his hammock until the crone straightened and vanished into the shadowy hold. When the crone was gone, the invisible presence released the first mate from his paralysis. Immediately, he leaped up and ran to his comrade, but the labored breathing and pale face of the second mate indicated that he was already past saving.

At dawn the first mate rounded up the remaining crew, and together they searched the ship from stem to stern. They found the old crone huddled asleep in the cargo hold. She'd made a nest behind two large crates that the men heaved aside. Around her bed were the waxen remains of black candles, one for each sailor she'd killed.

The first mate had the crone dragged in front of the captain. When the captain roared at her, she shook her ringed fingers at him and shouted back in a language that made the sailors' stomachs writhe and their flesh tremble, though they understood not a word spoken. The captain passed swift judgment on the stowaway who had murdered most of his crew. He had the crone dragged out on deck, lashed to a gun, and flogged. The crumpled body that fell to the deck little resembled a human, but the crone still managed to raise a ringed finger and point at the captain. For a moment her eyes glowed red, and the captain staggered as if shot. Then the crone collapsed in death, and the crew made haste to pitch her body overboard. The once-living bundle of blood and rags floated pitifully behind the ship. Even the sharks avoided it.

The captain, shivering and sweating by turns, managed to grab the arm of the surgeon before he passed out. "For God's sake, save me," he mumbled. But the surgeon could not. Already the captain's blood was thickening, his heart draining of its lifeblood. Within an hour he was dead.

That night a terrible storm rose out of nowhere, its heart centered around a tiny bundle of blood and rags in the sea. The depleted crew had no chance of survival against such a blast as this. All were resigned to their fate as the bow of the ship began its final climb up a towering wave too mighty to crest. When they pitched over backward, the first mate commended his soul to God.

He awoke to hot sun and salt-whitened skin. He was lying on his back on a piece of decking that bobbed a few yards from the western shores of Africa. Above him floated the glowing figure of the voodoo priestess. The mate recognized her at once. She was the presence that had awakened him in the night. "I have saved your life, *marin*, so you may spread the word," the priestess said. "Leave my people alone."

As she vanished, the first mate heard shouts coming from the shore. He raised his head and saw men wading into the water to fetch him to safety. When they carried him ashore, the first mate made a solemn vow that he would spread the word, as the voodoo priestess had instructed. And furthermore, he would never work on a slave ship again. He never did.

January 1, 1808. The importation of slaves was made illegal in the United States.

16

La Maison Mal

LALAURIE HOUSE, NEW ORLEANS

"Me, I do not like the new neighbors," my wife said, twitching the curtain back into place and coming to sit in her favorite chair before the fireplace.

I looked up from my newspaper. "Pardon, *cherie*. What did you say?"

"I said, I do not like the new neighbors," my wife repeated, shaking her head. "*Mais non.* That woman with her fancy paintings and her crystal chandelier and her fancy airs; all that gilt and glamour is a fabrication. There is something else there. Something cruel hiding behind her social mask. And her husband is worse. *Le médecin* [doctor] has the eyes of a demon."

I put the *New Orleans Bee* down on the table and gave my wife my full attention. Many years of marriage have taught me to trust her hunches. I have never known her to be wrong.

"What do you think is wrong?" I asked.

"I do not know," she replied, her dark eyes troubled. "It may have something to do with her slaves. They are too thin. And the cook, she jumps and cowers when she hears sudden noises or raised voices. I have heard that slaves in other colonies do this, but here in New Orleans we honor the Code Noir and

95

this should not be so. No slave should live in fear of torture or abuse. I do not like it."

"What do you think we should do?" I asked, troubled by her words. We owned no slaves and never would. I paid our servants handsomely and we treated them like family, for they lived side by side with us day and night and had helped raise our children.

"Watch and listen, for now," she replied, running her hands nervously through her long dark curls, barely brushed with silver. "And I will ask the *remedie* man to pray."

I nodded and sat back in my chair thoughtfully, making no move to pick up my paper. My wife only went to the remedie man when she was extremely worried about something. So I would watch and listen, as she instructed.

At first all I noticed were the number and variety of entertainments that were indulged in by the LaLaurie family. Balls and masques, dinner parties, soirees; le médecin and his madame seemed determined to outdo every host and hostess in New Orleans. But then I saw other things that made me uneasy. The cook rarely left the house, and when she came out into the yard, she limped as if her ankles were sore. One of our kitchen servants claimed that the cook was regularly shackled inside the LaLaurie kitchen. The girl had seen the chains when she went next door on an errand. Our servant was an honest girl who had never lied to us, and I believed her story.

I woke one night to find my wife standing at the window staring over at the LaLaurie house.

"What is it, chérie?" I asked, and she whispered: "I thought I heard someone screaming from the upstairs of *la maison mal.*" The evil house.

"Come back to bed," I called, and she came and curled up in my arms, her body trembling.

"Where are they, husband?" she murmured. "Where are her slaves? It takes many people to run such a grand house with so many parties, yet we see so few. And none of them attend the social dances at Congo Square."

"Or go to Mass," I agreed. "And they are a sickly lot, which is surprising since they are living in the house of a doctor."

"They are so shaky and thin. And their eyes haunt me," my wife replied. She was crying helplessly in my arms. All I could do was hold her close, wishing to weep myself. It was a lovely mansion with something rotten at its core, but what could we say? What could we do? You can't report intuition to the police.

The very next night there came an incident that we could and did report. I was searching for some old documents upstairs when I heard terrified screams coming from next door. I rushed to the window and saw Madame LaLaurie, red hair disheveled and face twisted with fury, chasing a young slave girl along the railed balcony. She held a whip in her hand, which she cracked again and again against the weeping child. From Madame's shouting, I gathered the girl had pulled her hair by accident while arranging the red tresses. The girl raced up to the cupola on the roof, tears of pain and fear streaming down her face as the whip lanced across her shoulders, her back, her legs. "I'm sorry. I'm sorry," the child wept.

Furious at such treatment, I tugged on the sash of the window, prepared to add my own voice to this discussion. The wood was swollen with disuse. I missed a key moment while I struggled, and it was only as the sash gave way and I thrust the window open, that I saw the child tumbling over the railing and falling down and down three stories toward the hard ground.

"*Mon Dieu,*" I cried in horror as I heard a soft thump as the small soft body impacted below. Death should sound louder than that, I thought numbly, watching Madame glare down into the yard. She straightened her hair and her bodice before striding back into the house and slamming the door.

I heard shouts below and saw that several of our neighbors had gathered in the street when they heard the shouting. My wife was among them, pale as snow and shaking. I rushed downstairs and swept her inside the house. "We have to report this," she sobbed, clutching the lapels of my coat. My wife held a cloth bag that smelled sweetly of herbs in her trembling hands. She'd obviously just visited the remedie man. I took the bag from her and summoned a maid to bring her tea and biscuits. The woman had served us most of her life and was more like a daughter than a servant. Her mere presence soothed and calmed my wife.

As I prepared a message for the police, I glanced out the window and saw two figures stealthily digging behind the LaLaurie house in the dim light of a darkened lantern. I recognized the shapes of the doctor and his wife. I shuddered. La maison mal. Evil house.

We were not the only neighbors to report the incident at the LaLaurie house. When the police investigated, they found the child's buried body, but the death was ruled accidental. "The child slipped and fell," Madame LaLaurie told the police and willingly paid the fine required by the authorities. Le médecin, her husband, remained silent and remote through the proceeding.

In spite of the rumors, the LaLaurie family continued to maintain their rank and standing in the community, and the lavish parties resumed. My wife would no longer go near the mansion. She had the driver of our carriage turn the other way, no matter how much time it added to her trips. "The house smells wrong," she told me. Mixed in with the smells of lavish food and expensive perfume wafted a baser scent: the stink of blood and urine and fear all mixed together. It turned her stomach. I never smelled it myself, except once when my carriage was nearly home and I saw a despairing face pressed against an upstairs window. It was there one moment and gone the next. But in that moment, a stomach-churning stench filled the carriage, and I nearly vomited.

That evening I asked my wife if there was anything the remedie man could do about the LaLaurie family. "He is working on a spell," she told me. "It will reveal all the hidden things about them so everyone can see what is wrong. But it is a big spell and will take much time to prepare and even more time to work. These things cannot be rushed, no matter how much we wish it so."

It was nearly a year after the terrible death of the child-slave that the remedie man's spell took effect. There was a fire in the kitchen of the LaLaurie mansion. The fire killed the chained cook—some claimed afterward that it was suicide—and began spreading through the house. The smell of smoke drew us into the street with the other neighbors, and we helped le médecin and his wife carry out the expensive paintings, the fancy furniture, the perfumed clothes. Then my wife, coughing painfully in the stinging smoke, cried: "Where are the slaves? Shouldn't they be helping?" Everyone stopped their rescue tasks for a moment and looked around. No slaves were present. Not one. Surely this could not be?

"They must be trapped in the house," a spectator cried. There were exclamations of horror from the watching crowd. Our neighbor, Judge Canongo, turned to the doctor and asked about the household slaves. Le médecin LaLaurie glared at the judge with eyes that were dull and lifeless like those of a zombie. Chills ran down my back as he said: "Never mind the slaves. Stick to the task at hand. And mind your own business," he added, thrusting a gilded chair into my arms.

But someone had already told the fire brigade about the missing slaves. A group of rescue workers—myself and the judge among them—raced into the burning house against the protests of le médecin and his wife. Up and up we ran, coughing and gasping in the smoke and heat of the fire. I was among the first to reach the top, remembering the miserable face I saw pressed to an attic window. We found the door barricaded against us and heard feeble cries coming from behind it.

"They locked them in," the judge gasped grimly beneath the handkerchief tied across his face. Coughing, teary-eyed from the stinging smoke, the men battered down the door with pickaxes and furniture, anything we could find. As the wood gave way, a terrible stench of fear, urine, blood, and decay roiled across our faces. To a man, we recoiled, and several vomited spontaneously in response.

"Mon Dieu, what is that smell?" gasped a man from the fire brigade. Grimly, hand clapped over my mouth, I pushed my way inside to find out.

The light was dim, and smoke already filled the rafters of the room. Dust, blood, and feces coated the steps, making them sticky underfoot. Then my eyes were level with the room, and for a moment I stopped dead, until the judge pushed me up the final steps. A crab woman in a cage writhed directly in front of me. I don't know what else to call her. Bones had been broken all over her body and reformed in strange positions. I tore my horrified gaze from her, hearing similar cries of disgust and anger around me. Another woman was strapped to a bed, part of her braincase exposed and writhing with maggots. Fresh urine dripped from under her bed, indicating that—evidence to the contrary—she was still alive. A severed head gaped on the table beside her like a foul lantern. Men and woman were chained to the walls. One man appeared to have been castrated and then given a woman's organs in exchange for his own. Some of the slaves had been skinned alive. Two were chained upside down. One man had his eyes sewn shut with strips of his own flesh. All stood or sat or lay coated with their own waste. Decay was everywhere, along with horrible instruments used to effect such terrible tortures upon these helpless victims. There was no hope in the eyes of any of the slaves in that room, in spite of the presence of rescuers.

Several more bodies were uncovered as we pushed aside our horror and focused on the practicalities of our rescue. Some of the slaves we could carry out. Others required stretchers. At least two died of their injuries as we attempted to move them from their torture chamber.

The crowd of fire watchers and rescue workers grew silent as the slaves were slowly carried out of the burning house, some still in shackles. The sight of the broken crab woman caused more than one person to turn aside in pity and disgust. During the turmoil the doctor and Madame LaLaurie vanished from view.

After the fire was out, news spread throughout the city about the evil discovered within LaLaurie House. Soon an angry crowd gathered in the street before the mansion. LaLaurie House was stormed and everything that remained of their possessions was destroyed, smashed to smithereens by the mob. A black carriage broke free from the yard as the crowd raged, with four horses galloping frantically through the melee. People scattered every which way to avoid their pounding hooves. I glimpsed the red-haired and tight-lipped visage of Madame LaLaurie as the carriage swept past.

The house, fire-gutted and mob-destroyed, was a ruined mess, an eyesore on our once-lovely street. Worse, the spirits of the many slaves who had died by the cruel hand of Madame LaLaurie and her doctor-husband haunted the ruin. I frequently saw the ghost of the little girl fleeing along the balcony and falling from the roof, her spirit caught in an endless cycle of fear and death. My wife woke often in the night, hearing moans and screams coming from the LaLaurie attic, and her maid encountered a skinned, chained slave coming out of the front door of the ruined house one evening as she was walking home from church. Within a month of the fire, our house was for sale and we were renting a ghost-free home across town.

We never saw Madame LaLaurie or her husband again. Rumor said the couple was hiding in France. We also heard that the new owners found a room full of skeletons when they began renovating the house, but I wasn't sure how much credit we could give to such a story.

There was one person, however, to whom my wife and I did give credence, and we owed him our thanks. Shortly after the fire revealed the truth about the LaLaurie family, we went to see the remedie man and we brought with us gifts of food, money, and my best hunting-dog pup.

"Thank you," my wife said simply, and I nodded to the elderly man as he stroked the head of the squirming pup.

"You're welcome, *mes amis*," he said, nodding to me in return.

17

The Casquette Girls

URSULINE CONVENT, NEW ORLEANS

The young Lady stood a little apart from the other *casquette* girls, who clustered together on the docks of New Orleans with their small trunks, known as *casquettes*, at their feet. They had been sent to the city from France to be trained by the nuns at Ursuline Convent and then placed in arranged marriages. It was a good chance for the young, flustered girls whispering together in the foggy evening air. French government had given them a dowry and offered them a new home in New Orleans to help populate the colony.

A robed figure in a nun's veil stepped into view, nodded to the chaperoning captain and his first mate and then called imperiously: "You are the new casquette girls, *oui*? Come with me. The hired porters will bring your casquettes."

The nun beckoned to a couple of longshoremen who stepped forward to take the girls' casquettes, most of which held a dowry given to them by the French government to sweeten the deal for their future husbands.

"*Un moment, Soeur,*" the Lady murmured, stepping out of the shadows. The nun was startled. She whirled and gazed uncertainly into fog as the pale young woman emerged into the lantern light, escorted by her small band of female followers. The Lady's swirling gray gown blended seamlessly with the fog. The effect—to judge from the sister's expression—was startling. She seemed to appear out of nowhere, this prepossessing young Lady.

"Our casquettes are too large for your hired cart, Sœur," the Lady said, gesturing toward several narrow boxes, each over six feet in length. The nun's eyes widened at the sight.

"Mademoiselle, those are not casquettes; those are coffins," she protested.

"Nonsense," the Lady said smoothly, nodding to her followers. Her Second already had several infatuated sailors in tow, and the men lifted the large casquettes and hauled them toward a waiting carriage as the leader took the arm of the startled nun.

Urging the sister toward the hired carriage where the casquette girls sat giggling uncertainly, the Lady gave a smooth non-explanation for the presence of six coffin-shaped casquettes, telling the nun that they were filled with the girls' dowry. The nun, mesmerized by her tone and gestures—rather in the manner of prey confronted by a snake—swiftly agreed that the Lady's casquettes should be placed in the safest place in the attic and should remain unopened, in order to secure such a valuable dowry from predation.

It was only when they entered the holy convent grounds that the hypnotizing effect lifted for a moment from the confused nun's mind. Her gaze sharpened, and she said accusingly: "Mademoiselle, you do not sound as if you come from *la belle France*. You speak with an accent."

"I have lived in Paris all my life," the young woman said calmly. "But my people came to France from . . . elsewhere."

"I see," said the nun. She gazed uncertainly into the Lady's eyes and once again fell into a trance, tugging agitatedly at her fingers until the carriage stopped at the entrance.

Her Second was already directing the sailors into the convent with the casquettes as the Lady and the French girls disembarked from the sister's hired carriage.

"Come in, girls, and welcome to your new home," the sister said, gesturing toward the front doors. The girls meekly followed the sister into their new home.

At the Lady's imperious nod, four of her followers trotted after them, folding their hands decorously and assuming piously innocent expressions.

"I will pay the sailors and see to a room for you, my Lady," her Second murmured with a bow. The young Lady nodded graciously and followed the sailors upstairs to supervise the delivery of the casquettes to their new dwelling place. As the last man departed, she knelt beside the tallest coffin and whispered: "Welcome to your new home."

The new casquette girls adapted easily into convent life. They attended daily Mass, did their chores, and took etiquette and other classes to prepare themselves to become wives. None of the French girls questioned the presence of the Lady or her comrades. All the young women had been strangers to one another until they stepped onto the boat in France. They did not even question the right of the Lady to commandeer the finest guest room in the convent, instead of sleeping in the dorm or in the small cells with the nuns. Even the mother superior accepted her presence as an honored guest rather than a true casquette girl. But still, the presence of the Lady made the nuns uneasy. And that was before the haunting began.

At first it was small things. Shutters banging in a windless night. Crops wilting overnight. Holy amulets melting. And all the girls' hand mirrors vanished. Sometimes a heavy weariness overtook the nuns and their casquette-girl wards so that they fell asleep over their books or kneeling at their prayers. When they awoke from such a sleep things were always slightly different within the convent, although none could say for sure what had changed.

The mother superior was worried. A shadow seemed ever present in this once-holy place, once renowned for its miracles. But what was its source?

Shortly after the new batch of casquette girls arrived, neighbors living close to the convent fell ill with a strange, wasting disease. They grew pale and listless. Some found odd puncture wounds on necks and wrists, as if they'd been bitten by an adder. But none died of snake poisoning. It was a mystery. It could not be yellow fever or another infectious disease, for none of the nuns or the casquette girls fell ill. This fact was soon noted around town, and the neighbors drew their own conclusions from these facts.

"Those French girls brought an evil curse with them from the old country," Monsieur Thibaut ranted one day after gaining entrance to the mother superior's presence.

"This is nonsense," the mother superior said stoutly. "They are a fine batch of girls and will make excellent wives. All of them attend Mass every day and say their prayers with us."

She faltered on the last sentence, picturing the line of coffin-shaped casquettes lying demurely on the upper floor of the convent. Then the mesmerizing blue gaze of the Lady, who sat beside the mother superior during meals, appeared in her mind's eye, turning her brain fuzzy and pink. The vision of coffin-shaped casquettes faded. "Utter nonsense," she reiterated severely and sent the neighbors away.

But Monsieur Thibaut was right; the mother superior knew it in her bones. Something was wrong at the convent. Whenever the mother superior spent a day away from the convent, feed–ing the poor or ministering to the locals, she felt an evil presence in the air as soon as she returned. It faded quickly as soon as she encountered the Lady.

The mother superior decided she must investigate this mystery before the reputation of the convent was destroyed completely by rumors of evil. One evening she went to the attic to break the lock on one of the mysterious coffin-shaped casquettes and look inside. To her surprise, the casquette was empty.

As she stared into its coffinlike depths, the Lady said from the shadows: "You know, *ma* Sœur, what they say about curiosity." A chill ran down the mother superior's spine. She looked over her shoulder and saw a pair of blue eyes glowing behind her.

Then a rush of wind blew open the windows of the musty attic. A dark figure swooped over the pane and landed beside the open casket. Now a second pair of glowing blue eyes took in the intruder. "*Bonjour, Maman,*" the Lady said. "We have a visitor."

The mother superior never knew exactly how long she was unconscious. She awoke in her bed with nuns fussing around her and the doctor opening a vein in her wrist to bleed the disease from her body. "*Mon Dieu!* We do not need any more blood around here," the mother superior cried feebly. She sent the doctor away and then ordered her nuns to permanently close the upstairs window with blessed silver nails. Confused but obedient, the nuns did as she asked. Satisfied, the mother superior fell into a healing sleep, only to be awakened by a blue-eyed visitor late the next day. She stared with loathing into the lovely face of the Lady bending over her.

"Do not nail the windows closed," the Lady said pleasantly. "It will not work. We have taken this place for our home. Your prayers and your blessed nails cannot drive us away. You invited us in."

"I never invited you in," the mother superior whispered, her voice hoarse in a throat suddenly gone dry.

"The day we arrived, your sister said: 'Come in, girls, and welcome to your new home.' So we came in," the Lady replied with a sweet smile.

"We will uninvite you," the mother superior said stoutly.

"You can try," the Lady said, straightening to smile at a casquette girl carrying a bowl of soup for the mother superior. "How lovely of you," she said to the girl. "The soup smells delicious. I am sure it will cure the mother superior very quickly."

As soon as the Lady departed, the mother superior sent for a priest and confided the tale to him. Shocked, he went upstairs at midday to see the coffins for himself. Upon his return he reported that all six were empty. The vile creatures they housed were roaming unhindered through New Orleans.

"We've tried nailing up the shutters with blessed nails, but this morning they were open again," the mother superior told him. "We don't have the strength to fight them."

"Try again," the priest advised her. "And all of us will pray."

They tried again and yet again. Each night they nailed the shutters closed using blessed nails and holy water. Each morning they found the shutters blasted open. The creatures were mocking them. It infuriated the mother superior and the priest. But what could they do?

At dinner one evening, a month after the empty coffins were discovered, the Lady's Second came hurrying in late with a sparkle in her eye. She bent and whispered something in the Lady's ear. Then she hurried out again.

The Lady turned graciously to the mother superior. "I have good news for you," she said. "My Second has found us a permanent home here in the city. My people are moving our casquettes as we speak. I thank you for your hospitality, ma Soeur. It has been . . . refreshing."

Daintily she touched the serviette to her lips and placed it on the table. "I must supervise our departure. Please stay and continue your meal, Mother Superior. It has been a pleasure doing business with you." At the door, the Lady turned and gave a small, mocking bow. "Don't try to find us," she said. "The consequence would be quite dire." She vanished into the hallway. Four "casquette" girls silently folded their napkins and followed their mistress from the room.

With their departure, the cloud lifted from the minds of the resident nuns. To a woman, they dropped their utensils and gazed in horror at one another, finally realizing the truth. Vampires had come to New Orleans.

18

The Doctor

NEW ORLEANS PHARMACY MUSEUM

My husband Tim booked us on a long weekend getaway to New Orleans as a last hurrah before our first baby was born. I looked forward to spending time in the Big Easy, with its historic French Quarter, fine dining, and festive air. We set out after work on Thursday, and a few hours brought us into the city. Tim had found a fantastic bed and breakfast at a great price, and when we told them it was our last hurrah before the baby arrived, they gave us the fancy honeymoon suite at no extra charge.

"Here are the honeymooners," our host said with a smile as he brought coffee to the breakfast table in the morning. A fellow-guest blinked at my obviously pregnant form and said: "Honeymooners?"

"In this case, it should be called a *second* honeymoon," I said calmly, hand on my round belly. "Our *first* honeymoon took place three years ago."

The man opened his mouth to make a joke but was nudged into silence by his wife. "Is it a boy or a girl?" she asked.

"It's a boy," Tim said proudly, taking my hand. "Timothy Junior. Four weeks and counting, right, sweetheart?"

"And boy do I wish we were done already," I complained, fanning myself with my napkin. "We need to plan more carefully next time. Having a baby in the middle of a hot Louisiana summer is no picnic."

The wife nodded in emphatic agreement.

As we lingered over coffee, the couple told us some of their favorite sightseeing spots in the French Quarter. They waxed particularly enthusiastic over the New Orleans Pharmacy Museum, so we added it to our list of adventures. We parted company reluctantly, and I waddled upstairs for a bathroom break before we went exploring in the French Quarter. Many happy hours of shopping and sightseeing ensued.

After lunch, Tim and I made our way to the Pharmacy Museum. Tim had his DSLR camera with him, since the couple had particularly raved about the beauty of the courtyard. I felt a little queasy as we stood staring up at the building. My eyes kept straying to a small carriageway on the left side of the museum, and every time I looked at it my nausea increased. I rubbed my tummy and grimaced uncomfortably.

Tim looked at me in concern. "Are you okay, honey?" he asked. "Would you rather go back to the inn and take a nap?"

"No, no. I'm fine. Probably something I ate," I replied. I'd grown used to the discomforts associated with pregnancy and saw no reason to postpone a pleasant experience since we were already here.

We entered the building and paid the entrance fee. As soon as I stepped inside, I knew this visit was a mistake. I am not psychic, but the bad vibe I received from this building was so strong I wanted to turn and run. It felt as if a pair of malevolent eyes had suddenly fixated upon me and their owner intended me harm. I stood frozen in the doorway of the main room, which was crammed full of old medical merchandise: bottles, signs, instruments, cases. Every inch of space was taken up with paraphernalia of all kinds. The room was a lot to take in under normal circumstances, and my current situation was far from normal. My nausea had returned stronger than ever, and I leaned against the doorjamb, swallowing stinging bile from my throat. In my mind I could picture a white-coated figure standing behind the glass cases mixing voodoo potions that I knew instinctively would not be beneficial to me or my unborn son.

Tim was already roaming through the room, exclaiming delightedly over old-time patent medicine bottles and dried herbs, taking picture after picture with his camera. "Come look at these surgical instruments, honey," he called over his shoulder when he saw me clinging to the doorway. He raised the camera and took my picture in the doorway. "I'm sure glad they don't use these anymore!"

The dark atmosphere in that room was so thick it was hard to breathe. Sun was shining through the windows, but it gave no cheer as I struggled past crammed cases and objects stacked on the floor. With every footstep I could feel a black shadow keeping pace with me. I was panting noticeably by the time I reached my husband's side. He took another picture of me as I approached. After viewing my face through the lens, his smile faded and he took my hand. "Are you in pain? Do you need to sit down?" he asked in concern.

"I'm okay," I said irritably. "Let's skim through the rest of these exhibits, and then you can buy me a cup of tea at that little bistro we passed."

Reluctantly Tim agreed to this plan and went back to taking photos of the exhibits, while I stared grimly at some tonsil extractors and tried to ignore whatever it was that was staring at me so fixedly. *Go away*, I thought at the dark presence. But it didn't move.

To his credit Tim tore himself away after another five minutes, and we headed upstairs to look at the exhibits on the second floor. I almost didn't make it to the top of the steps. It was like climbing through a dark tunnel in a deep cavern far below the earth. A hollow whistling sounded in my ears, and my husband's voice seemed far away. Only the click of the camera penetrated the gloom.

I could hardly see as we emerged upstairs. "Here's the birthing room," Tim called excitedly. "Come look, honey. This is where you'd have been a hundred years ago."

I stepped across the threshold and screamed. A doctor in a white coat covered with blood was walking straight toward me, his hands full of ominous medical instruments. There was an evil half smile on his face that told me he employed some very heinous practices. Behind him I thought I saw a woman on the bed, writhing in agony. Then a terrible pain struck through my abdomen and I crumpled to the floor, the world going dark.

I don't remember much about the next few hours. When I regained full possession of my faculties, I found myself in a New Orleans hospital and a real modern-day doctor was telling me to push. Twenty minutes later Tim Junior was born and placed in my arms.

In the excitement of the new birth and the inherent lack of sleep that goes with new parenthood, I forgot all about our abbreviated visit to the Pharmacy Museum until the day Tim loaded his pictures onto the computer. I was rocking the baby to sleep in his bouncy chair when my husband gave a shout of surprise from the office. I'd never heard that tone from my even-keeled husband and raced into the study. Tim Junior woke when he heard the ruckus and started wailing from his bouncy chair in the next room. My husband pointed at the screen. "Look. Oh gosh, honey. Look."

I looked.

On the screen was the picture Tim took of me leaning on the doorjamb. Standing a foot away from me was the semi-visible figure of a blood-stained doctor; the same man I'd seen in the upstairs birthing room. I gulped and then leaned over Tim's shoulder and advanced the photos using the keyboard. Yes, the doctor was there again, walking next to me as I crossed the pharmacy floor toward my husband. And a few more mouse clicks showed a huge orb in the center of the birthing room where I'd fainted.

"Gosh almighty," Tim swore. "No wonder you fainted! I'd better look into this. Make sure there are no aftereffects to you and the baby."

I nodded faintly and staggered to the living room to pick up my squalling son.

That evening, after researching the topic on the Internet, Tim told me some of the stories circulating about the museum. Apparently a Dr. Dupas had practiced medicine in the building, and people had a reputation for disappearing mysteriously under his care. It was rumored that he experimented upon pregnant slave women, giving them voodoo potions and other experimental medicines that often left mother dead and infant dead or disfigured. The outside carriageway that had so disturbed me was the place where the wagons stood at night, waiting to receive corpses from the doctor's failed experiments.

Tim clutched me close to him during this explanation as if he'd never let me out of his arms again. "I should never have taken you there," he moaned into my hair.

"It's okay, honey," I comforted him. "I'm fine. The baby is fine. How could you possibly know that the Pharmacy Museum was haunted by an evil baby doctor?"

"We are never going there again," my husband said firmly.

On that point, we both agreed.

19

"Aidez-Moi"

"Aidez-moi."

The cry woke him out of a sound sleep. He sat up abruptly, sure that he'd heard a maiden's voice calling for help. He rushed to the window, left wide-open on this hottest of summer nights to catch any stray breeze off Lake Pontchartrain.

He found it ironic that he, a man deathly afraid of water since birth, should own property on the lakeshore. But he had inherited the house from a bachelor uncle, so the price was right. And he liked to hear lake water lapping on the shore at night. It was soothing. When the breeze came from across the lake, as it sometimes did, then this was the coolest place to be in summertime in New Orleans.

He strained his ears, listening for any sound. The water murmured along the shoreline, sounding forlorn. A tiny breeze played with his long hair, brushing a strand across his nose so he sneezed; a raucous sound on this still night. It made the singing night frogs cease their buzzing song. All was silent. And then he heard it again: "Aidez-moi. *S'il vous plaît,* aidez-moi." (Help me. Please, help me.) A woman was sobbing out on the lake.

119

What was she doing out there? Had her boat caught on a snag? Had it capsized and left her adrift on the remains? Grim possibilities flashed through his mind as he leaned farther out the window. He called: "Mademoiselle, where are you? How can I assist?" There was no reply. Perhaps she could not hear him.

He strained his eyes, trying to see across the large lake. The crescent moon hanging low in the sky did little to assist his searching gaze. The wind buffeted his face, whistling urgently in his ears. The tiny crackles and buzzing of night creatures was noticeably absent from the night. He heard it again: "Aidez-moi." Sobs. It was unbearable.

He withdrew from the window, threw on some rough clothing, and hurried outside, wondering what he should do. His uncle had left him a small dory. It stood dry and forlorn beside the shed. He had never in his life gone out on the water. Indeed it had taken great fortitude for him to pull the dory onto dry land and place it beside the shed. All his life his mother had warned him against the water, saying: "The *remedie* man, he told me: 'If you go out on the water, you will surely die.' So stay on land, son. Stay on land."

But he could not, in good conscious, ignore a woman's cry for help. He was a gentleman, and he would assist her, or die trying. Grimly, he went to the dory and started dragging it toward the water. His body trembled when he felt the first waves lapping his shoes. No! He could not go near the water. He could not.

"Aidez-moi," the woman's sobbing voice rang from across the water, louder now. "S'il vous plaît, aidez-moi." The cry shook his heart.

A strong breeze howled around him, forcing him backward toward land. Oh how he wanted to obey the wind. He wanted to step back onto dry ground. Wanted to return to his soft bed. But he could not.

For a moment he saw his dead mother's face before him. "Stay on land, son. Stay on land."

Then the woman's sobs grew louder, filling his ears, breaking his heart. "Aidez-moi!"

He tossed the oars into the dory, pushed it fully into the water and leaped aboard. "I am coming, mademoiselle. I come!"

He rowed determinedly toward the sound of sobbing, though he had trouble at first with the oars. But he'd watched enough fishermen in his time to understand the principle, and soon he was skimming across the lake, listening for a woman's voice. The water was much shallower to the right of his home, according to local fishermen. That was where he'd find the woman; he knew it in his bones. Her boat was caught on an underwater mudflat or a snag. But soon she would be free.

"Aidez-moi," the cry was quite near now. He risked a look over his shoulder, hoping to see the troubled maiden. But the lake appeared empty. Bewildered, he ceased rowing and turned around completely to look across the water in the dim light of the crescent moon. Where was she? Was she trapped in the water? Perhaps her skirts were held down by seaweed or stray timber?

"Aidez-moi," the cry came again, on the far side of the dory.

A glimmer of light flickered across the waves from the crescent moon as he plunged across the dory, causing it to sway dangerously.

"Aidez-moi."

He clutched the gunwale and looked over the side, directly into a foul green face filled with needle-sharp teeth. Green hair streamed around a twisted face. The creature's eyes glowed with a red light that had nothing to do with the crescent moon. Her striped tongue licked across tattered lips as the *coquin l'eau* (evil water spirit) stretched impossibly long, scaled arms out of the water and yanked him down into her embrace. He had time for only one scream before they vanished with a swirl beneath the surface of the lake.

The man's bloated body floated ashore two days later. From its tattered appearance, the fisherman who found the corpse assumed some large fish or maybe an alligator had feasted on his flesh before he drifted toward land. The man's mourning family sometimes wondered how their relative came to drown, since he never went near the water. But they never found out. Only the old remedie man knew the truth, for he'd seen it all in his scrying bowl on the day the boy was born.

20

Pool of Blood

She took the first-floor apartment in the Lamp Factory because the rent was so cheap, even though the old mansion in which the factory resided had a dubious reputation. But she was a poor widow, forced to earn her living as a seamstress, and she could not be picky about where she lived. Any apartment—even one in a haunted factory—was better than the street. She was a lucky woman, the seamstress told herself repeatedly as she moved her few belongings into the tiny flat.

It was a nice little place. The sounds from the factory rarely penetrated the apartment, and no one lived upstairs, which was a bonus to her way of thinking. Too often the seamstress had lived in places where the upstairs neighbors kept one awake at night. After a week in her new dwelling, the seamstress was feeling pleasantly at home. There was plenty of light from the windows to accommodate her sewing needs, and the factory workers, when she encountered them entering or leaving the premises, were polite and friendly.

It was one of the women workers who told her the ghost story associated with the seamstress's new home. It happened during the Civil War, when the Union Army occupied New

Orleans under General Ben Butler, that two Yankee soldiers stole some army funds. Their crime was discovered, and the soldiers in blue fled from their barracks and hid themselves in the mansion. They stole food from neighboring homes and occupied their time counting their stolen money, swapping stories, and singing Union songs like the "Battle Hymn of the Republic." But the authorities were closing in on their hiding place. When they were found, both men would be executed for their crime. So when they learned that troops were closing in on their hiding place, the two renegade soldiers lay down side by side on the bed, and each placed a revolver over the other's heart. At the count of three, they both pulled the trigger. When the army men burst through the door, they found two corpses lying on the bed and a pool of commingled blood dripping onto the floor below.

"Folks still see two soldiers in blue staring out of the upstairs windows above the factory," the woman said to the seamstress. "Right up there," she added, pointing to the window directly above the seamstress's apartment. "That's where they died."

"Good heavens," murmured the seamstress, nonplussed. "Have you ever seen them?"

"Not me. I don't believe in ghosts," the factory work said. "But one of the night watchmen claims he can hear the soldiers striding around up there at night singing the 'Battle Hymn of the Republic.' "

"That's unfortunate," said the seamstress.

The seamstress pondered the ghostly tale all afternoon as she sewed. Finally she shook it off. It was ridiculous to worry about a couple of Yankee soldiers who died many years ago.

That night the seamstress was shocked awake by the sound of heavy footsteps above her. Were the ghosts walking around up there, she wondered, sitting bolt upright in bed. Her heart thundered painfully beneath her ribs as she listened to someone pacing the upper floor. Then she remembered the worker's story about the night watchmen. Of course, it was the watchman doing his rounds. How silly of her to imagine a ghost! The seamstress lay back down and drifted off to sleep. Above her, a man started whistling the "Battle Hymn of the Republic."

By the end of the second week of her tenancy in the factory apartment, the seamstress had reconciled herself to the nighttime pacing and whistling of the night watchman. It only happened once or twice a night, and it comforted her to know that someone was keeping away the robbers and other notorious characters that sometimes peopled the streets of New Orleans. She completely discounted the story of the Union ghosts. It was rubbish to believe in ghosts.

She was working hard on a lovely white satin wedding gown for the eldest daughter of her best client that day. The first fitting was next week, and she was determined to have the dress ready by then. She sewed diligently all morning, sparing only a few moments to have a simple lunch before taking up the dress again.

The seamstress had reached a particularly delicate piece of sewing, involving a yard of very fragile lace, when she was distracted by a drip falling onto her neck from above. A second and third drip wet her neck and head as she jerked upright. Where had the water come from? It wasn't raining outside. And even if it were raining, what of it? The roof on the mansion was solid. Nothing had leaked last week during the big thunderstorm. Two more drops fell on her head and neck. Impatiently she wiped them off with her hand. Then the seamstress's eyes widened in shock. Her fingers were covered with blood.

At that moment several more red drops descended from the roof, plopping onto the wedding gown in her lap. Now that she was no longer focused on one small portion of the gown, the seamstress saw red drops were scattered all over the white satin. Taking a shaky breath the seamstress looked up at the ceiling. Her eyes popped open in astonished disbelief. Directly above her chair a huge pool of blood was leaking through the boards of the ceiling, creating a huge, ugly smear. As she stared in horror, mouth dry and skin prickling, a drop broke loose and fell onto her nose.

The seamstress screamed when the blood touched her face, and screamed again as the temperature of the room suddenly plummeted, turning the dripping blood into particles of red ice. Ghostly footsteps marched up and down above her head, shaking the floor. "Glory! Glory! Hallelujah!" two male voices bellowed through the roof. Then their song was interrupted by two loud shots, fired at the same time.

Abandoning the wedding dress, sewing machine, and all her belongings, the bloodstained seamstress ran screaming from the house. She pelted down the street and only paused to look back when she reached the relative safety of the corner. In the window above her apartment, two shadowy men in blue uniforms with bloody gaping holes in their chests waved merrily at her. The seamstress gave a piercing shriek that set all the local dogs to howling, hooked a right at the crossroads, and ran pell-mell until she reached the safety of her cousin's house across town.

After hearing her tale, the cousin's son was sent to fetch the seamstress's belongings, and the cousin offered her a home until she could find a less-haunted apartment in which to live.

For many years following the seamstress's abrupt departure, factory workers continued to see two Union soldiers gazing down at them from the upper window. And the night watchman still reported the sounds of two soldiers marching around the second floor at night, singing the "Battle Hymn of the Republic."

No one stays long in the first-floor flat at the factory. For each year, on the anniversary of the soldiers' death, a pool of their mingled blood leaks through the boards of the upper floor and rains down upon the head of anyone foolish enough to be renting the apartment underneath.

21

It's Just a Costume, Right?

BOURBON STREET, NEW ORLEANS

New Orleans has always been a Mecca for my spouse and me, living as we do in the backwoods of Louisiana. After a rough year we both decided we needed a special treat, so we took time off to visit the city for Fat Tuesday and the Mardi Gras festivities. Like the other locals, we steered clear of the French Quarter, choosing instead to focus on the family-friendly parades in other parts of the city.

For the big Sunday night Bacchus Parade, we marked out a spot on St. Charles Avenue near the beginning of the parade route and sat wrapped in a blanket people-watching until the big event started at 6:00 p.m. The crowd loomed elbow to elbow, with children lifted onto shoulders or perched on ladders, eager to see the fabulous floats in one of the biggest parades of the season.

How do you describe Mardi Gras parades to someone who has never seen one? With its carnival atmosphere, breathtaking floats, gaudy costumes, and marching bands, the spectacle of the Bacchus parade defied description. Our favorite floats were all here. I loved the Officers float, called New Orleans and All that Jazz. And who could resist the Bacchagator—a 105-foot, three-piece float of a green alligator? My wife Jill loved the

Kong floats—King Kong, Queen Kong, and Baby Kong—and the 85-foot-long mammoth Bacchus whale.

"Throw me something," Jill shouted to every passing float, bouncing on her toes and clapping her hands like a little kid. And they always did! We quickly gave up trying to put all the beads we collected around our neck. They would have knocked us over. Fortunately I still had the plastic bag that housed our long-eaten lunch, so we had someplace to store our Mardi Gras treasure.

Some out-of-state visitors got so excited that they jumped in front of Jill to grab a stuffed animal thrown to my wife by a float-rider. I pulled her back soothingly before she got too riled and whispered: "There's always another float, honey."

"Oh, yeah," she said, looking mildly embarrassed.

I once made the mistake of reaching down to pick up a doubloon that fell through my hands and nearly lost a finger to one of the local kids, who was snatching up everything at street level. I laughed and decided to put my foot on anything else that fell to the ground. I could always pick it up between floats.

When the magic was over and the crowds dispersed, Jill said: "Let's go to Bourbon Street for a drink."

I eyed my wife dubiously. The French Quarter at night during Mardi Gras season was full of pickpockets and people behaving in a risqué manner. Not something I thought she would enjoy.

"Oh, come on, we're adults. We can handle it," Jill said. "And it's not Fat Tuesday, so the crowd won't be quite so rowdy. We can't come to New Orleans for Mardi Gras and not visit Bourbon Street."

"We can go shopping on Bourbon Street tomorrow when the rowdies are sleeping it off," I suggested mildly. But I could see Jill was going to be stubborn about this. For the sake of marital harmony, I gave in. We packed our belongings into the car and drove to the French Quarter for a late-night drink.

It took quite some time to find parking, but finally we made it out into the packed streets. Bunting and decorations were everywhere, which gave the French Quarter a festive air. But the crowd was a different matter. Here, the costumes were scanty and revealing, many tourists were drunk, and the streets were filled with detritus. It was hard to move around in the crowd, and the mood was wild. Jill edged closer to me and kept her purse under her jacket to keep it safe from pickpockets. I could tell she didn't like this crazy celebration any more than I. We were quiet outdoors people, not city folk, and the family-friendly Bacchus parade was more our style.

Above the roar of the crowd, I heard a strange wailing sound, something between the howl of a dog and the cry of a baby. It gave me goose bumps whenever I heard it and made me want to flee the area for safer climes. The howl came again, closer this time. Jill gripped my bicep with trembling fingers and whispered: "What was that?"

"I don't know," I said. Then the crowd eddied and parted for just a moment. Ahead of us, we clearly saw a small twisted figure with red eyes, a forked tail, clubbed feet, and stubs on its head that might have been small horns. It looked like a miniature devil. My eyes met those of the creature, and I broke out into a cold sweat, every nerve in my body singing, "Danger, danger!" Then the crowd surged forward and the figure was gone.

"Th–that was just a c–costume, right?" Jill gasped into my ear as a mime lurched past.

"Lord, I hope so," I replied, steering my wife around a couple of scantily clad visitors and into the nearest pub. We pushed our way to a quiet spot at the back and ordered drinks, which I for one needed desperately after my glimpse of that . . . whatever it was.

A grizzled old fellow sat at a single table beside us, nursing a mug of beer. He gave us one keen, all-seeing glance and then returned his attention to his drink. But he must have noted our pallor, for he said casually, in a Cajun-accented voice: "*Mes amis*, are you well? Too much Mardi Gras, perhaps?"

Jill glanced over at him, and I could tell she liked his looks. Jill is half Cajun and she understands the nuances of the culture.

"We just saw the scariest costume," she said. "It was a miniature devil with glowing red eyes and small horns on its forehead. It gave me quite a turn, monsieur." Her hand shook at the memory, spilling a few drops of beer on the table.

"Ahhh," the old Cajun whispered, staring down at his mug. "And were you sure it was a costume, *chérie*?" he asked my wife.

Jill carefully set down her mug. "I hope it was a costume, monsieur."

"The devil's child, he is a very old New Orleans legend," the old Cajun murmured reminiscently. He sipped thoughtfully at his beer and then told us the following tale:

Many years ago a lovely Creole girl married a wealthy plantation owner, and they had many daughters together but no son. When the Creole girl became pregnant yet again, she went to a voodoo priestess and begged for her help in bearing the much-desired son. However, the plantation owner, unbeknownst to his wife, had once cheated the voodoo priestess and she was glad of this chance to be avenged upon him. The priestess cursed the Creole girl's unborn baby and declared that it would be the devil's child and not that of her plantation-owner husband.

As the time for her delivery approached, the girl had a series of nightmares that left her awake and trembling each evening. In her dreams she saw a small twisted figure cradled in her arms. The Creole girl was terrified by the dreams, afraid something horrible would happen to her unborn son.

Scarcely a fortnight later, the girl went into labor and was brought to bed in the family's town house on Bourbon Street. Her child was born on Fat Tuesday, and he had a twisted visage, horn stubs on his forehead, a forked tail, and clubbed feet. The Creole girl bled to death before she could behold her newborn son, but the sight of the devil's baby drove her husband mad and he was locked away in an asylum.

At first, the Creole family was able to keep the baby hidden. But the child truly was the son of the devil. He grew with preternatural speed and strength. Soon he broke out of his confinement and began haunting Bourbon Street and its surrounds.

"They say that the spirit of the devil's child still roams the streets of the French Quarter around Mardi Gras," the old Cajun man said in conclusion. "Sometimes at night people hear him howling in rage and pain."

I shivered. Jill grabbed my hand and whispered: "*Merci*, monsieur, for telling us this story." I felt her fingers trembling in mine.

"You are welcome, chérie. Be careful when you walk at night on Bourbon Street," the old man replied.

"We will," I said fervently and went to settle our tab.

22

Forty-Nine Beaus

NEW ORLEANS

He was a fledgling reporter, just learning the trade, so naturally his editor never gave him the good assignments. But he was a handsome boy, with a charming manner and flashing smile that made girls dizzy, so he was frequently sent to cover the "human interest" angle. Ladies loved to talk with him, and even the gents unbent before his witty tongue.

Today's assignment was a piece of cake, the reporter reflected as he strolled toward his destination. The last scion of one of the original families was turning ninety-five, and she had graciously given the newspaper permission to conduct a personal interview. She was the daughter of one of the dons who came to the colony in 1770, shortly after France gave control of Louisiana to Spain to pay a war debt.

The reporter was composing interview questions when he rounded a corner and got his first look at the don's mansion. He stopped and stared, appalled by the dilapidated mess of grandeur fallen on hard times. Someone should pull the eyesore down, he thought, staring at the sagging roof, the rusting ironwork, the weed-stricken yard.

The reporter had to tussle with the ironwork gate. It reluctantly opened with a banshee's screech that raised every hair on his body. He shuddered past moldering piles of junk and clawing weeds and climbed unsupported up the rickety steps, afraid to touch the splintered rail for fear of catching a disease from the slime.

It took a long time for anyone to answer his knock. Finally the warped portal creaked open and a bent old servant peered cautiously out into the daylight. The servant looked the reporter over from one angle then shifted about a foot to the left and looked him over again. Then the wrinkled eyes peered blurrily over the reporter's broad shoulders. Finally the man whispered: "It looks like the coast is clear. You won't bring in any ghosts, will you, young Master?"

Ghosts, the reporter thought disbelievingly.

"No, sir, I won't bring in any ghosts," he told the old servant, tempted to pat the man reassuringly on the shoulder of his wilting, dusty uniform. The old servant tottered backward, swinging the door wide, and the reporter stepped into the gloom of glory long gone. The once-magnificent wallpaper and tiling was now coated with mildew and cobwebs. The servant's footprints could be seen in the dust on the floor. He'd evidently come from a room in the back, probably the kitchen, given the smell of cabbage and boiled meat wafting down the passage. The servant must be fixing the old lady's lunch.

The air in the house was frigid, unbelievably so, given that it was midsummer. The reporter shivered and wondered how they kept the house so cool as he followed the old man up a groaning flight of stairs. Surely they didn't have money to buy ice, given the decrepit state of the house and grounds.

A chill breeze swirled around the reporter as he climbed. He shuddered, wishing he'd brought his winter coat.

The reporter sneezed three times as he entered a tawdry boudoir, his nostrils twitching at the smell of decay and dust and ancient perfume. The room looked as if it belonged in the red-light district, with its cheap decorations and lewd air of seduction. His eyes swept right past the heap of rags in the burgundy armchair, searching for the grand lady he'd come to interview. Then the servant announced his name, and the rags stirred. The reporter turned his gaze disbelievingly on the old woman who opened filmy dark eyes to look at him. The rags were actually a faded *quinceañera* dress covered in dust. The sparkle on her thinning scalp was a tarnished tiara, and the baubles in her ears and around her neck were probably priceless family jewels, though neglect had faded their elegance. There was a ring on every finger of her withered old hands, with string tied around the bands to keep them on her bony digits.

The old woman had no teeth and there was no beauty in her sucked-in cheeks and wrinkled skin. But a spark kindled in the old eyes, and the reporter saw that the bones of her face and body were slim and elegant. Hard to believe that this tiny woman that looked ready to fall apart was once a beauty, but the signs were there if you looked carefully.

The senorita cackled with delight when she laid eyes on the handsome young man. "Come in, come in, senor. Welcome to Casa Rosa. You are an appetizing specimen, I declare. I think I should have you for dinner tonight." She erupted with laughter, almost choking on her wit. Then just as swiftly, her mood shifted and she screamed at her servant to leave them alone and prepare for the grand supper that she was giving that night for all her beaus. "Including this new one you've brought me," she concluded, simpering at the reporter.

He masked his revulsion and took the chair the senorita offered, hiding behind his notebook until his face was back under his control. The room was stuffy and suffocatingly hot, as if all the summer warmth had been channeled into this one tawdry boudoir, leaving the rest of this sinister house cold and restless and unhappy. The reporter shook away the thought. He was not given to fanciful notions, but this place . . . and this ancient woman . . . disturbed him. Something about the old woman's eyes made him want to run from the room. But he had a job to do, and so he started asking questions of the withered creature in the burgundy armchair. When was she born? What was it like in the days under the Spanish rule? How had New Orleans changed since then?

It was uphill work. The senorita wanted to talk about her father the don, who was once an important man with money to burn. According to the reporter's preliminary research, the don died shortly after the senorita turned fifteen, but the ancient crone spoke of him as if he were still alive.

Then she talked about her Spanish beaus. Oh, how the men came courting her! She'd danced every dance at her quinceañera, and there'd been many more balls and grand suppers. And intimate dinners, too, she hinted with a simper and a flutter of filmy eyelashes.

"The gifts the men would bring me! Jewels and expensive cloth and fancy foods," she sighed. "They all wanted me. Half a hundred men. No. Only forty-nine men. I am just shy of fifty beaus, though we can fix that at dinner tonight, handsome man."

The reporter nodded with a pasted smile on his face, wondering what the senorita was talking about.

"Of course, none of my men ever left this house," the senorita continued, piercing dark eyes suddenly filling with a wicked red glow that made his heart pound heavily in his chest.

"Never left?" he croaked, hand shaking so badly that he almost dropped the pencil. "What do you mean, senorita? Your beaus never wanted to leave because you were so beautiful?"

"They never left," she crooned, stroking the rings on her fingers and rocking back and forth in the burgundy armchair. "I was the one they desired. My beauty enchanted them until they could talk of no one but me. Each time a man was overcome by desire for me, I invited him up to this very room to partake of my beauty. For them, there could never be another woman. Once they tasted my delights, how could anyone else measure up?" The sinister red light in her eyes grew more pronounced as she fixed her eyes on the reporter again. "No other woman could have one of my beaus. It would be . . . sacrilegious. So my beaus never left Casa Rosa. I made sure of that. They are—all of them—still here."

She stopped rocking suddenly and gazed at him thoughtfully. "I always wanted fifty beaus. Fifty is such a nice number. Half of a hundred. Forty-nine beaus were never quite enough. I didn't think another man would visit my boudoir at my time of life. But here you are, senor. Handsome and young and fit. You are worthy and should be allowed to partake of my beauty, just as the forty-nine who came before you. We will have dinner tonight, just you and me. And afterward . . ." She started to laugh again, and the light in her dark eyes grew stronger.

Suffocating waves of perfumed air washed over the reporter as she spoke. He felt dizzy in the heat of the room. Or was it the heat of her gaze? *She's mad*, the reporter thought, chills running all over his skin. *I must get out of here!*

The senorita shifted in her chair as if about to rise, and his heart leaped into his throat. What if she pulled a knife? She looked too decrepit to do him harm, but insanity lent strength to the smallest of people, or so he heard. Then her head flopped to one side and she was suddenly asleep. She snored once, twice.

The temperature in the room dropped precipitously, as if the heat were somehow fueled by the senorita in her dusty quinceañera dress. The reporter leaped to his feet, dripping with the sudden sweat of relief. He must get away at once, before the mad creature awoke. He raced for the door, but the handle wouldn't turn. The servant had locked him in! The reporter cursed and flung all of his weight against the door. He was afraid the sound might awaken the senorita; afraid of what she might do to him in her insanity. But he had to escape! He took a few steps back and kicked the door. His foot went through the wood near the handle. He thrust his hand into the gap and unlocked it from the outside.

As he raced into the hall, the reporter felt a wave of heat from the room behind him. A querulous voice called for her servant, for her father, for her beau. In his panic, the reporter turned the wrong way and nearly slammed into a shimmering figure clothed in the Spanish garb of yesteryear. The translucent young man had a sad face and luminous eyes.

Good God, there really was a ghost! The reporter felt himself gibbering in fear. The spirit grabbed the reporter's arm with ice-cold hands and tried to drag him down a slimy back staircase toward the rose garden at the back of the house.

"No," shouted the reporter, flinging himself backward. Ice-cold wind whipped around him, and for a moment he was overwhelmed by the stench of rotting flesh and a vision of forty-nine white faces writhing around the hall, reaching for him with spirit hands. "Join us," they crooned.

Screaming, the reporter wrenched away from the specter and raced for the staircase, flinching at the blast of heat from the boudoir where the old lady still called for her servant. He whipped through the dust and the cobwebs and mildewed splendor of the decrepit mansion as the old servant doddered from the back kitchen to answer his mistress. The servant held a tray with two wineglasses and a decanter. *Probably full of poison wine*, the reporter thought with a hysterical laugh. He burst through the warped front door and ran down the littered path toward the gate. And skidded to a halt. A ghostly figure in full evening dress stood in his way. The ghost gave a mocking bow and swung the gate open for the reporter. Then it split in half as if cloven in two by an ax. Each half fell on either side of the open gate.

The reporter levitated off the ground and sped through the gate in two bounds. He was halfway across town before he realized he'd left his notebook at the old mansion. Never mind. He would buy another and would fabricate some kind of interview that would satisfy his editor. Great God in heaven, that was a narrow escape.

Shortly after this interview the reporter was asked if he wanted to cover the crime beat. He refused. A year afterward, the senorita died and her house was sold. When the new owners started renovating the mansion, they found numerous skeletons buried beside the north wall of the rose garden. All were male and all had died quite young. The forty-nine unfortunate beaus of the senorita of Casa Rosa.

23

Mon Ami, Loup-Garou

GOVERNOR NICHOLLS STREET, NEW ORLEANS

Jean-Claude Dubois waited patiently for his wife Priscilla to descend from the carriage before alighting into the lamplit street before the cathedral. The elegant woman beside him gave a sudden bark of laughter and said: "Pierre chose the place for his nuptials well, *je pense*. This is a place of mixed heritage if ever I saw one!"

"As mixed as we are, *chérie*," Jean-Claude agreed smoothly, lifting her hand to his lips as the moon shone brightly overhead.

Suave and sophisticated, the head of the Dubois clan had traveled far from his home just outside Montreal to attend this wedding. As a young man, Jean-Claude was a frequent visitor to the United States, actively pursuing the family business throughout the whole of North America. Then his father died and Jean-Claude became head of the Dubois clan. His duties changed overnight, and his travels outside Canada were few and far between. This New Orleans trip was a real treat for himself and his beloved spouse, or it would be after they took care of a little business for Pierre.

For all his Acadian roots, Pierre was a still a distant member of the Dubois clan, with all the unique gifts this entailed. The clan was very careful about their marriages, so Pierre had written to Jean-Claude to ask his permission before he wed his Creole sweetheart. In response, Jean-Claude and Priscilla had arrived a few days prior to the wedding to inspect the girl and meet her family. The girl they had liked instantly. Proud, spirited, and lovely, she was deemed worthy to bear the name Dubois. Her twin brother was another matter.

At first the brother was friends with Pierre Dubois, intrigued by the apparent sophistication of the Acadian man from the back bayous. But when Pierre started courting his sister, the twin turned surly and suspicious. It took much of the sparkle from the time of courtship, for the girl Antoinette loved her twin as well as Pierre, and it saddened her that their friendship had soured.

"I do not understand it, *mais non*," she told Jean-Claude over dinner last night. "They had such good times together. Anton, he said Pierre was special, which is why I was eager to meet him. But now he hates Pierre, and he will not tell me why."

"Jealousy takes many forms, *ma fille*," Jean-Claude said soothingly. "Anton has had your love exclusively for many years, and now your brother must share you with his friend. You will not have so much time for Anton when you are a wife and mother. It is the way of the world, and your twin must accept it."

The girl's lovely dark eyes widened. "*Moi*, I never thought of that. It would explain so much!" She took a spoonful of consommé and swallowed thoughtfully. "*Oui*, it makes sense, Monsieur Dubois. *Merci*. Your insights relieve my mind."

"We are family, my dear. Please call me Jean-Claude," he replied with a smile. This was a high honor, and Antoinette understood it as such. She blushed and smiled warmly at her soon-to-be cousin-by-marriage.

The two families parted amicably after their initial meeting. Late that night Priscilla and Jean-Claude discussed the matter of Anton. "He suspects something," Priscilla told her husband. "He was rude to me in the most subtle ways over dinner. Nothing overt, but it was there nonetheless. Anton knows he is walking a fine line."

"He has crossed the fine line," Jean-Claude said crisply. "I will take care of it, chérie."

Priscilla nodded in satisfaction.

Pierre and Antoinette had chosen St. Augustine Catholic Church in New Orleans for their wedding. Coming from such a speckled background himself, Pierre found the history of the church irresistible. It was a lovely building with a mixed congreg–ation in which free people, slaves, and Creoles worshipped pew by pew, if not actually side by side. A few months before the dedication of the church, the freemen and -women began purchasing pews for their families. Challenged, the Creoles tried to buy more pews than the free folks. Ultimately the "War of the Pews" was won by the free people, who bought three pews for every one pew purchased by their Creole neighbors. In addition to their own pews, the free people gave all the pews on both side aisles to the slaves as their exclusive place of worship. This mix of the pews resulted in the most integrated congregation in the entire country: one large row of free people, one large row of Creoles, and two outer aisles of slaves.

"If people were so tolerant in Montreal, we need not live in the shadows," murmured Priscilla to her spouse as they joined the queue entering the church through candlelit doors.

"Things will never be that liberal, chérie," Jean-Claude said gently. "And there are . . . advantages to living in the shadows."

The couple split apart at the door. Priscilla went to support Pierre's parents on the groom's side of the aisle while Jean-Claude slipped into the pew just behind the bride's family, where he could watch Anton unobserved. In a flurry of fine music, the ceremony began. The blushing bride was radiant as she came down the aisle. Only Anton's angry face cast a shadow as the lovely words of the wedding ceremony rang through the church.

At the moment the priest asked if there was any known impediment to the marriage, Jean-Claude clapped a hand over Anton's opening mouth and spirited him out the door with supernatural speed. No one, not even the bride's mother sitting inches away, noticed what happened.

Out in the chilly churchyard, Jean-Claude released the man, and they glared at each other by the light of the moon. "I know what you are," Anton cried angrily. "*Loup-garou!* Werewolf. I will tell the world! I will not have one such as you marry my sister!"

Anton raced toward the side door of the church then fell to the ground under a mighty blow. He rolled over and gasped as Jean-Claude loomed above him. Jean-Claude had paused halfway through the change so that his upright form was more man than wolf. Long incisors gleamed in the moonlight, though his face was still recognizably human. Hair sprouted along his arms, and claws were already visible at the ends of his hands.

"I could kill you right now," Jean-Claude growled. "It would give me great pleasure. Our family has suffered for many centuries under such intolerance as you have displayed this evening. But it would give my new cousin pain, je pense, to lose her twin brother on her wedding day. So I have a different plan for you."

"What are you going to do?" Anton gasped, sweating with fear in the moonlight.

"I am going to make you one of us," Jean-Claude said with a fang-filled smile. Anton cried out in horror, and then the jaws of the master loup-garou closed on his throat.

Anton was missed from the receiving line but showed up rather drunkenly at the reception that followed the wedding Mass. "Anton started drinking early," the bride's uncle observed to his sister. No one, save Pierre, noticed that Anton's cravat was thicker than normal to hide the bloody bandage around his neck. During a lull in the proceedings, Pierre glanced questioningly at Jean-Claude, who smiled grimly and nodded confirmation.

"You have a new student," he murmured in his cousin's ear as they walked toward the carriage waiting for the Dubois party just outside the reception hall.

"*Mon ami*, loup-garou," Pierre replied softly.

The bridegroom smiled and the moonlight reflected off slightly elongated incisors. Then Antoinette floated through the door to say farewell to her new cousins and Pierre was human again, absorbed instantly by the lovely woman at his side.

"*Très bien*," said Priscilla, nodding approval to her husband as they settled into the carriage. "A job well done."

24

The Death Tree

He had escaped at last, God be praised. His older brother the prince would never cease searching for him, he knew. But it would never occur to his brother that he, Sulyman, would leave the Middle East; would abandon his people and go to live among strangers in a heathen land. So America was the perfect place to hide.

Sulyman sent his most trusted servant to scout this foreign city called New Orleans, where his ship had landed. "Go and find a place for me to settle with my wives and children and their families," he commanded. So the servant went into the city and searched for a place to live. He returned within a few hours with good news: A plantation owner had retired to the country during the lean years of the Civil War and had a large house available for rent on Dauphine Street. All the people Sulyman had brought with him into exile would fit into the residence with ease. The deal was soon struck, and Sulyman moved into the mansion with his wives, children, servants, slaves, and various family members who had accompanied him to America.

The Americans were agog with curiosity at the exotic garb and strange manners of the new family in town. Some explanation was needed, but Sulyman did not feel the need to be honest with these strangers. In truth he was a man on the run from certain execution, for had he not stolen gold, jewels, and the prettiest of the wives from his brother the prince? But for the benefit of the neighborhood, Sulyman claimed to be the sultan himself, come with his family and possessions to live a life of freedom in America.

He could tell that the people of New Orleans did not approve of him or his people. So be it. The money stolen from his brother provided him with wealth beyond their dreams and helped pay for this new American life. Let them gossip. It did not matter what they thought of him.

Meanwhile Sulyman decided to turn his new residence into a palace worthy of the one he had left behind. The servants were hard at work for the first several months, redecorating the mansion to Sulyman's standards. Ironwork was placed on entrances to the doors and windows, and a harem was constructed in which to house his many wives and their children. All four stories were refashioned in the style of the Middle East to remind Sulyman of his lost home. And two eunuchs stood guard over his front door night and day. The latter were the source of much interest in the neighborhood. Sightseers from all over town strolled or drove down Dauphin Street just to see the eunuchs and the exotic Middle Eastern palace they'd heard about.

Time passed not unpleasantly in this new life. As Sulyman relaxed into his new role, he began throwing lavish parties full of music and opium and incense to entertain the locals. The lifestyle he took for granted at home seemed exotic and decadent to the people of New Orleans. He couldn't tell if they were thrilled or appalled by his entertainments. Truth to tell, he really didn't care what they thought. In idle moments Sulyman wondered how many of his neighbors he could convert to his religion. It would be comforting to have people of like belief around him in this foreign land.

Two years passed and Sulyman grew careless, letting down his guard and giving too many clues to his true identity when he entertained at his elaborate parties. He supposed it was inevitable that rumors of the exotic sultan of New Orleans would reach the ears of his brother the prince, who would never cease to hunt for his traitor brother while breath remained in his body.

In the wee hours of the morning, Sulyman woke to complete and utter silence in the mansion. Even at night his household was full of the soft footsteps of servants; giggling or sharp arguments from the women and children in the harem; the smell of opium; the clinking of glassware or dishes being served or cleaned up. Someone was always awake in the house, even in the small hours of the morning. The utter silence made every hair on his body stand on end. The assassins were here. Oh, yes, he was sure of it. His brother had found him at last and had sent his men to execute the traitors that had followed Sulyman into exile. The assassins must have been watching the household for days and would have this execution planned down to the last detail.

Sweating in terror Sulyman slipped out of bed, grabbed his knife, and slid into the hallway, still in his dressing gown. He didn't know if his brother planned to kill him here in America or have him dragged back to the Middle East to face judgment there. Whichever way this played out, Sulyman intended to go down fighting.

His bare foot encountered a warm sticky substance a few steps from his door. Sulyman expected to see a body in the dim light coming from somewhere downstairs, but there was just a liveried shoulder and an arm lying in a pool of blood. He swallowed bile. They had hacked the servant to pieces. He saw body parts strewn all over the hallway.

The assassins were toying with him, he realized. They could easily have swept into his bedroom and killed him in the time it took them to dismember this servant. Fear clutched his gut. His children and his wives were in the harem upstairs. Would his brother spare them?

He already knew the answer, but he forced himself to walk upstairs anyway. Blood seeped under the door of the closest room. He checked it, choked, and hurried to the next room and then the next. His wives were all dead. Dead and dismembered, like the servant. The nursery was the worst. He vomited at the sight of the beheaded small bodies that represented his last hope for the future.

Sulyman knew assassin eyes were watching his every move as he grimly checked each of the family rooms and then went down the servant's staircase to the ground floor. Family dead. Servants dead. He found his two eunuchs lying in a puddle just inside the front door. The stench of their blood mixed sourly with the smell of incense and opium. Everyone was dead. Except him.

Though he was expecting it, Sulyman's heart still jumped with fear when sudden light spilled through an open door at the back of the room.

"Greetings, old friend," a familiar tenor voice murmured. Sulyman turned to face his brother's chief assassin. "I apologize for our tardiness," the assassin continued. "It took us many months to track you. I am most displeased by this ineptitude and will understand if you wish to . . . lodge a complaint with the prince." The assassin bowed, one hand over his heart.

"We have brought you garb more appropriate to this occasion," he continued as one assassin disarmed Sulyman from behind and another grabbed his arms. A third man appeared from somewhere on the right and mockingly held up traditional funeral garb. Sulyman shouted with rage and fought like a tiger as the men stripped off his clothing. A blow to the temple stunned Sulyman just enough to make him docile while they dressed him for the grave. Then the assassins dragged him out to the courtyard. A few flickering candles marked a hole underneath a twisted tree. Several men stood waiting there, holding shovels.

"No," gasped Sulyman, understanding at last the fate his brother intended for him. They were going to bury him alive! "No!" he cried again as his body was shoved unceremoniously into the grave.

Sulyman hit the ground hard, but panic cleared his head as nothing else could do. Heart racing, he flipped himself over and tried to climb out of the hole as the first shovelful of dirt cascaded down upon him. The assassins worked rapidly in utter silence, throwing dirt onto Sulyman and shoving him ruthlessly down whenever he tried to scramble upward. It was terrifying how quickly the dirt piled up around him, encasing his legs, his torso, his neck. When Sulyman tried to scream, the chief assassin threw a shovelful into his mouth.

Sulyman thrust his hand out of the thickening mass surrounding him, trying to grab the shovel and pull an assassin—any assassin—down into the grave with him. The chief assassin laughed softly, and the dirt flew faster and faster until it covered Sulyman's mouth and nose, suffocating him.

He could still feel the fresh air on his hand long after the dirt covered the top of his head, but when he tried to breathe, he sucked in dirt and had no room to spit it out. Sulyman felt the chief assassin pat his hand.

"Good-bye, old friend," the man said, his voice sounding muffled through the dirt covering Sulyman's ears. Panting through his nostrils in the rapidly disappearing air, Sulyman muttered a curse against his brother the prince. But there was no one left to hear him. He was alone.

25

Voodoo Queen

The night thrummed to the sound of drums beating, beating, beating. Figures chanted and danced around the flickering firelight. Flecks of color danced on the waves of Lake Pontchartrain as sparks flew up from the fire, where the mighty cauldron bubbled. Before them the Voodoo Queen danced to the music, holding up a snake while spectators numbering nearly twelve thousand individuals crowded the lakeshore to observe the ceremony. And in the shadows under a live oak tree a young girl stood watching.

The wind rustled the leaves above Louisa's head. Beside her, *Maman* stood still as a statue, observing the mighty St. John's Day voodoo ceremony. Louisa was ten years old, and her mother had brought her to the city to meet Marie Laveau, the famous Voodoo Queen.

Louisa felt a soft tapping on her ankle. She responded instantly to the touch, bending down and holding out her arm. A snake curled lovingly around her wrist and slithered upward as the girl straightened. It was a medium-size cottonmouth. She cradled him in her arms, and he wrapped his tail around her waist. "Good evening, Dan," she murmured, stroking his soft side.

Before the fire, the Voodoo Queen froze mid-dance. Her eyes searched the night for something . . . someone. . . . The bonfire flared suddenly, lighting two figures under the live oak tree. The Voodoo Queen stared straight at Louisa, who was cradling a large cottonmouth in her arms. Slowly, the Voodoo Queen lowered the snake in her arms until he, too, was cradled against her chest, mirroring the girl. As Voodoo Queen and child stared at one another, the chanting of the crowd faltered and stilled. One by one, the dancers turned to look at the girl under the tree.

"Come," Maman said to her daughter. "We will go now to the house on St. Ann Street and speak with the Widow Paris." Maman bowed to the Voodoo Queen and Louisa followed suit. The dancing and chanting did not begin again until mother, daughter, and Dan the snake had vanished into the shadows.

As they made their way into the city, Louisa pondered what she had seen on the lakeshore. Her great-great-grandmother had been a Vodun priestess back in West Africa, long before the white man stole her people away to be slaves in Haiti. Her many-great-grandmother's powers were legendary. She could heal with a glance and curse with the flick of a finger. Any standard religious ritual performed by the priestess was ten times as powerful as that of any ordinary witch doctor. Her magic was so strong that any object she held in her hand glowed afterward for a year and a day; so said the tales passed down through the family. Even now complete strangers told tales of the priestess's healing powers that had saved the life of one or more of their ancestors.

Though the gift of magic passed down through each subsequent generation, it never again bloomed as strong as that of the West African priestess. Still, it was much stronger than that of any ordinary mortal. Members of the family became powerful Vodun practitioners living in Haiti or the Americas. They lived simply and kept their faith secret, for they were part of the first circle of worship, called by oracle to the very highest levels of the Vodun religion.

Louisa's father lived in Haiti as a child until he was sold to a plantation owner outside New Orleans. He married several years later. His bride was a religious woman who practiced voodoo faithfully, though she had no magical gifts of her own. For a long time the couple thought they would have no children. Then the woman conceived and gave birth to a baby girl. Such was her travail giving birth that the midwife said she would have no more children. It saddened the couple, but they were glad to have been given one child as a special gift from the Vodun spirits and the other elements of divine essence that govern the Earth.

The new maman was disconcerted the first time she stepped out of the small slave cabin that she shared with her husband and found it surrounded by snakes, weaving and tumbling all over themselves to look through the small window at her new baby daughter. Her husband—himself a powerful witch doctor in the family tradition—knew what it meant. Their only child, come to them so late after so much travail, had inherited the mantel of the long-ago princess. She was a Vodun priestess from birth, a healer, a magician, a wise woman. And who knew what else she might become in time?

Louisa spoke the old West African tongue before she spoke French or English. It seemed as if she learned it out of thin air. By the time she was a month old, Maman was resigned to finding snakes occupying Louisa's bed each morning. The crib had been hand-carved with animals and holy Vodun symbols by her doting papa. He added a frieze of snakes to the mix as soon as he realized that his daughter's gifts were as strong as that of the long-ago priestess.

As soon as she could walk, the child went to sit each day by the Mississippi River, listening, listening, listening. . . .

"What do you hear, child?" Maman asked her when she was old enough to articulate the thoughts in her mind.

"Everything," Louisa said, cradling a baby snake that crawled into her lap as she sat in silence by the river. "The water and the breeze, they tell me everything."

To her parents it seemed as if every Vodun spirit—a hierarchy that ranged in power from major deities governing the forces of nature and human society to the spirits of individual streams, trees, and rocks—came at one time or another to speak to their only child. Animals living on or near the plantation came to her, too: the alligator and the heron; the egret and the wild pig; the dog, the cat, and the horse. Louisa learned their secret names and their hidden ways. A black rooster followed her everywhere like a puppy dog and never seemed to mind the constant presence of snakes.

Papa knew his daughter should not grow up as a slave. She was a force for good in this dark world and must be free to pursue the path in front of her. He and Maman worked night and day to earn money to buy their freedom. By the time Louisa was five, they were living on their own little property and her father had more work than he could handle as a healer, while Maman supplemented their income with her skilled dressmaking. The little family prospered.

The faithful of the Vodun religion often stopped by the little cottage in the bayou to visit with Maman or consult Papa. They left small gifts and offerings before the family altar and watched the little girl who could hear the loa (spirits) speak to her and knew people's secrets because the wind and the water whispered them into her listening ears.

On Louisa's tenth birthday, Papa told his wife: "I have taught Louisa all I know about gris-gris [amulets]; about herbs and healing; about power and the loa spirits. My gifts are limited. Her gifts are boundless. If we were in Haiti or Africa, she would already sit in the first circle of worship with the great priests and priestesses of our faith. But we are here in America. What more can we do for her?"

Maman replied: "I think we should take her to meet Marie Laveau."

Marie Laveau, the famous Voodoo Queen of New Orleans, was reputed to have great gifts. She was born around 1800 and married Jacques Paris at St. Louis Cathedral when she was twenty-five. When her husband disappeared after six months of marriage, she became known as the Widow Paris. A year later she became the common law wife of Christopher Glapion and had some fifteen children by him.

As a young woman, Marie Laveau worked as a hairdresser of high-society ladies among the Creole of New Orleans. But her skills in voodoo were much in demand, and she soon became the first commercial voodoo queen, specializing in romance and finance. Her services were sought out by both practitioners of the religion and by members of high Creole society. She even opened some of her voodoo ceremonies to the public. The people of New Orleans both craved and condemned the ancient ceremonies of healing, dance, and purification rites, which they did not understand. As the years passed, Marie Laveau's reputation spread throughout Louisiana. She was said to be all-knowing and all-powerful, a faithful friend to the poor and repentant and a feared enemy to those who opposed her.

Since voodoo as practiced in New Orleans was a blend of traditions in which voodoo deities were closely paired with the Catholic saints, Maman was not certain if it was proper for the family to consult with the famous queen about Louisa's gifts. The family strictly adhered to the tenets of West African Vodun, which did not include Catholicism. Was Marie Laveau the proper person to tutor their daughter in the old ways?

Maman had kin living in New Orleans who had firsthand knowledge of the Voodoo Queen, so she consulted with them regarding Marie Laveau's qualifications. Her kinfolk assured Maman that Marie Laveau had deep spiritual gifts and her relationship with the loa was thought to be as strong as that of the ancient priestesses of West Africa. So it was decided. The family would travel to New Orleans for the St. John's ceremony on Lake Pontchartrain, and they would introduce Louisa to Marie Laveau.

The drive to New Orleans took many days. The little family arrived on St. John's Eve and spent the day visiting with relatives of Maman, who were their hosts in the city. All three planned to attend the voodoo ceremony the next evening, but Papa was called away unexpectedly to tend an emergency illness, so only Maman and Louisa went to the lakeshore to worship with Marie Laveau.

Their kinfolk told Maman that it would probably be the Voodoo Queen's daughter that presided over the St. John's Day ceremony, and so it proved. After observing the ceremonies for more than an hour, Maman made the decision to leave. They would consult with the Widow Paris while Marie Laveau the younger finished the St. John's Day rituals.

Louisa was tired and sleepy by the time they reached the house on St. Ann Street. She cuddled Dan close to her heart, suppressing a yawn as Maman knocked on the door. She wondered why Maman was certain someone would be home on this important night. Shouldn't they all be at the ceremony? A light flickered in the window, and then the door swung wide. Maman murmured something to the figure in the entrance, and the young woman motioned them within.

Louisa came awake at once when she crossed the threshold. The air in the house seemed to shimmer around her. She heard a clear high-pitched note like a wet finger rubbing the rim of a fine glass: joie de vivre, joy unbounded. Dan perked up and lifted his head.

"Simbi," Louisa murmured. "Erzuli."

Maman glanced at her sharply. Louisa smiled; her face was alight with happiness. Maman relaxed. It was right to bring her daughter here. This house was a temple.

The young woman led them to a small chamber where a wrinkled old woman lay peacefully on the bed, propped against several pillows. The woman's eyes were closed, but she was not asleep. She held a small rattle in her hand, and they could hear her humming.

When Louisa stepped into the room, the woman's dark eyes snapped open. Woman and child stared at one another for a timeless instant. Then Louisa bowed.

"Madame," she murmured. She turned slightly to one side and bowed again to the empty air beside the bed. "Legba."

Abruptly the pillows underneath the Widow Paris heaved. A dark head poked out from under the cloth, followed by a long, thick body. Dan perked up and weaved back and forth, welcoming the newcomer.

"Zombi," Louisa said.

"Zombi," Marie Laveau agreed.

The high-pitched note in the air grew louder, and power crackled on every surface until Maman felt her hair stand on end. The young woman caring for the elderly widow backed out the door, her eyes wide with fear. Maman followed, leaving the two Vodun healers alone with the loa.

Maman and the young woman, who was a Laveau granddaughter, sat drinking tea by the fire during the long hours of the night. Inside the bedroom they heard the murmur of voices punctuated by the occasional beat of a small hand drum or the shake of a rattle. Once Louisa giggled. As if summoned by the sound, a black rooster flapped through the window and landed beside the bedroom door. It rapped impatiently on the wood with its beak. Louisa let it into the bedroom and then swiftly closed the door.

At dawn the bedroom door swung open of its own accord. Maman and the granddaughter stood abruptly, like soldiers at attention, as a semi-visible force swept past them and banged open the front door. Zombi the snake and the black cockerel followed at the heels of the crackling power.

Glancing into Marie Laveau's bedroom, the two trembling women saw Louisa kiss the Voodoo Queen on the cheek. Then the girl and her cottonmouth came into the main room to rejoin her mother. With a sparkling smile, Louisa took Maman by the hand and they followed the loa through the open doorway into a day filled with transfiguring light.

"Thank you, Maman," Louisa said.

26

The Zombie

CHALMETTE BATTLEFIELD AND FORT ST. PHILIP

The whole room stank of fear and death. The voodoo *sorcier* stood in the doorway of his small home, unable to move as his eyes took in the blood splattered everywhere. It filled the cradle in the corner and spattered across the wooden table where his wife prepared and served the meals. There was blood on the log walls and pooling under the bed where his wife's nearly decapitated body lay amid the rags that were all her attacker had left of her clothing. His wife would have resisted the invader with all her strength, and so perhaps her death made a sordid kind of sense. But why had the attacker killed the baby? Had he tried to purchase the wife's obedience by threatening the baby?

Grimly, the sorcier waded through the blood to the box where he kept his herbs and gris-gris. He must retrieve the tools he used for his divination. He would find out who had done this terrible deed and exact his revenge upon them. It had to be an outsider who killed his family. All the Creoles, Spanish, and Americans in the vicinity knew the reputation of the voodoo sorcier. None would tempt his wrath, fearing a swift and brutal revenge.

Chief among the sorcier's suspects were the British soldiers that had anchored their ships at Pea River in the mouth of the Mississippi. The British forces came ashore at the mouth of the Bayou Bienvenue and an advance guard had captured the Villere plantation, only a few miles away from the sorcier's cabin. The American general Andrew Jackson sent a fourteen-gun schooner downriver to bombard the British positions, while General John Caffee tried to halt the British soldiers on the river. The Americans had some initial success, but ultimately the British lines held and Jackson's men withdrew to defensive positions along the Rodriguez Canal.

For the last two weeks, the two sides had been preparing for their next battle. The British were scouting the Mississippi River, digging canals and building earthworks all through this area. One of their soldiers must have found the sorcier's lovely wife alone in the cabin and taken liberties that had ended in this brutal massacre. Grimly, the sorcier went to the private altar he had set up in the woods and began the divination ceremony that would show him the face of his enemy.

At dawn on January 8, 1815, the British began their assault on the American lines. The British soldiers gallantly attacked, but the Americans were well prepared, and their artillery wreaked havoc on the advancing soldiers. The British general tried to rally his men and continue the assault despite the fact that two horses were shot out from under him, but he was mortally wounded and died on the battlefield. The battle at Chalmette was quickly concluded. The Americans had won the day.

The sorcier's divination told him that the British soldier he sought was not among the ground troops at this battle. The soldier was a messenger currently stationed aboard the fleet to act as a liaison between the naval and ground commanders. The sorcier's visions also indicated that a naval battle was imminent following the British troop's defeat at Chalmette, and so he went to Fort St. Philip and signed on as a volunteer.

True to his vision, the British commander Vice Admiral Cochrane ordered yet another attempt on New Orleans. This time, the vice admiral decided to attack Fort St. Philip with those ships of the fleet that could pass the shallow mouth of the Mississippi. On the day following the defeat at Chalmette, the British sent four ships up the Mississippi to commence fighting. At 12:00 a.m. on January 9, 1815, the Royal Navy approached the fort, formed a line of battle and made preparations for a bombardment. At 1:00 p.m., the fort's signal station was abandoned and partially burned by the American troops, who wanted to leave nothing for a fast-approaching British shore party. The sorcier's enemy was among those assigned to the landing party.

During the ten days of bombardment that followed, a chain shot removed the luckless murderer's head and he was buried in a shallow grave by the shore. After firing a thousand rounds, the British gave up their plans for New Orleans and retreated from the area, leaving the body of the murderer behind.

The voodoo sorcier was not a forgiving man. He was not content with mere death for his enemy. Oh, no, the man's suffering had not ceased with this death. Quite the contrary. Shortly after the British retreat, the sorcier dug up the body of the decapitated soldier and carried the already-rotting corpse to the voodoo altar near his home. Calling upon dark powers known only to a few of the masters, the sorcier dragged the man's spirit back into the withering body, reanimating it. The late British soldier became one of the living dead—a zombie.

Unlike other zombies, the head of the soldier was not reintegrated with his corpse. In order to see where it was going, the British zombie was forced to carry its head under one arm as it walked the banks of the Mississippi River in its bloodred uniform, doing its new master's bidding.

The good people living along the river road were terrified when the zombie first appeared among them. It strode briskly down the main street of a local town in its bloodred uniform while horses reared, women screamed, and the local priest stood on the doorstep of the church frantically waving incense. The zombie carried a carved figurine in its hand. When it mounted the steps of the local mercantile, all the shoppers retreated to the corners of the room (and a few jumped out the window onto the boardwalk below). The zombie placed the figurine on the counter before the merchant, who owed the sorcier money for a health charm he'd purchased over a month ago. The man took one look at the zombie and fainted. His wife, also terrified but more levelheaded, ran upstairs and returned with the sum in question. She placed it on the counter and retreated while the heavy hand of the zombie fumbled for the cash. Finally it raised its bloodstained severed head until the head was eye level with the counter. Thus oriented, the zombie was able to pick up the money and direct it into a pocket. It then wheeled with military precision and marched out of the shop, down the street, and into the bayou.

It might be conjectured that the sorcier would lose business due to the presence of such a terrifying servant. But the river folk were enamored of the power that the sorcier displayed in the creation of such a zombie. He became the most popular voodoo witch doctor on the river. People from all walks of life consulted him for love potions, health remedies, curses, and cures of all kinds. All gaped in wonder at the red-uniformed zombie standing guard outside the sorcier's small cabin while his master sold gris-gris and remedies. Any person who didn't pay on time could expect a visit from the sorcier's servant. The merest hint of a bloodred uniform appearing on the local streets sent folks running for their money purse.

A year after the battle of New Orleans, the sorcier saw a lovely young woman walking down the main street of the town and fell instantly in love with her. His contacts told the sorcier that the girl was called Virginie and that she was betrothed to the local blacksmith, whom she had known from childhood.

Determined to have Virginie for his own, the sorcier sent the zombie to the house where she lived with her parents. In its free hand, the red-coated zombie carried a bouquet of flowers and a bag of the most expensive sweets available at the local mercantile. Virginie's mother hid under the table when she saw the zombie march into the yard. Virginie, who was chopping wood, stared wide-eyed at the romantic tribute held out to her by such a terrifying figure. She pointed a trembling finger at a large stump on one side of the yard. The zombie carefully turned its head in its free hand so it could see where the girl was pointing, and then marched to the stump and laid down flowers and candy with an audible thump. Then the zombie whirled with precision and stomped away.

Thus began the courtship of Virginie. The zombie appeared every day with a new present for the girl: herbal remedies, food, fancy scarves, handmade jewelry. The sorcier had accumulated much wealth thanks to the presence of his zombie, and he lavished it with abandon upon the object of his affection. Virginie was upset by the attention. She did not know the sorcier. She did not love the sorcier. She was not engaged to the sorcier. Why was he causing her so much embarrassment? If he wanted to court her, why send the zombie? Why not come himself?

Her betrothed, the blacksmith, was infuriated by all the unwanted attention paid to his future wife. Every day his clients crowded into the smithy to tell him what new gifts were brought to Virginie by the zombie. Each evening the blacksmith would stop by Virginie's home and glare at the rapidly accumulating gifts atop and surrounding the stump. Neither Virginie nor her parents dared throw them away for fear of incurring the sorcier's wrath.

"He wants to marry you," the blacksmith told Virginie one evening, two weeks after the zombie's first romantic call.

"He can't marry me. I am betrothed to you," she replied. But her eyes flickered to the pile of gifts in the yard, and she shivered. The sorcier could force her hand with one of his love potions. Or—even easier—he could ask her terrified parents for her hand in marriage, and they would grant his petition just to get rid of the zombie.

"Maybe we should get married right away—tonight. Then the sorcier couldn't force himself upon me," Virginie said urgently. "I am sure the priest will help us."

"I am sure he won't," a deep voice said smoothly from the path outside the house. The blacksmith and Virigine turned. The red-coated zombie stood at attention by the gate, its head watching them alertly from under its arm. Beside it, the sorcier stood in his best clothes, holding a bouquet of flowers and a bottle of wine.

"I am obviously the better suitor, my dear," the sorcier continued smoothly, advancing into the yard. "Your parents will tell you so, if they can be persuaded to come out of the barn. I spoke to your father this afternoon, and he gave me his blessing."

"You have no right to steal my betrothed," the blacksmith roared, rising to his impressive height and flexing strong, muscled arms. "Virginie is mine."

"Take care of the blacksmith, Zombie," the sorcier said, stepping up to Virginie and handing her the flowers.

The zombie marched forward, and the blacksmith took a swing at its chest. It was like hitting a tree. The zombie did not even stumble. It raised its free arm and slapped the blacksmith in the face. The blacksmith flew across the large yard and struck the side of the barn with a massive thump. He slid down to the ground, unconscious, a rapidly bruising handprint on his face.

"You monster," Virginie shouted, throwing down the flowers and racing to the blacksmith's side.

"The priest has agreed to marry us at twelve o'clock this Sunday, right after Mass," the sorcier said pleasantly, smiling infatuatedly at the girl on her knees beside the unconscious blacksmith. "If you aren't there, my zombie will fetch you. Good night, Virginie."

Summoning his servant with a casual wave, the sorcier strolled down the path and disappeared into the bayou.

Virginie's parents crept out of the barn. Together they carried the blacksmith into their small home and revived him. The next day the blacksmith went to the city of New Orleans to consult with a voodoo queen regarding the sorcier and the zombie. He returned home with a plan, which he relayed first to Virginie's frightened family and then to the local priest.

The wedding day arrived, and so did Virginie in her best dress. The blacksmith sat sullenly at the back of the church, his face disfigured by the zombie's handprint. After Mass, the priest motioned for the congregation to remain seated. At precisely twelve o'clock, a massive blow from the zombie opened the front doors. The sorcier strolled down the aisle, trailed by his bloodred-uniformed best man. Under its arm, the zombie's blue eyes darted this way and that, as if fascinated by the frozen audience in the pews.

The priest motioned for Virginie to join them at the altar and began the words of the wedding Mass. During the prayer Virginie removed a small packet from her pocket. When the priest said "Amen," she ripped it open and threw the contents directly onto the severed head of the zombie. As salt and sacred herbs rained down upon it, the priest grabbed a vessel full of holy water and threw it over the bloodred uniform. The zombie found its voice for the first and last time. It opened its mouth and screamed as smoke poured forth from its head and torso. It writhed in agony as the imprisoned soul fought to get out of its tormented body. Then the zombie wheeled and scuttled swiftly from the church as the congregation choked and coughed in the acrid smoke that filled the room.

"Get out," the blacksmith said softly into the sorcier's ear. He'd walked silently from the back of the church to the man's side while they were distracted by the zombie. "What we did to the zombie, we can do to you. You are not the only one with voodoo powers."

The sorcier glared up at the massive man and then fled after his smoking zombie.

The priest motioned for the congregation to open the windows on either side of the sanctuary. Once the smoke was clear, he began the wedding Mass for the second time and married Virginie to her blacksmith, to the delight of all present.

Back at his cabin on the bayou, the sorcier did his best to repair his injured zombie. "All I wanted was someone to love," he grumbled. "I lost my wife and my son thanks to you. I deserve another chance at happiness."

The zombie rubbed its burnt face with its free hand and did not reply.

At that moment they heard a hesitant tap on the open door. "Monsieur le sorcier, are you home?" a lilting alto voice called. The sorcier sprang from his chair and went to the entrance. Standing there with a basket on her arm was a very pretty young woman. She had a plump round face and sparkling dark eyes. "My mother sent me to buy a remedy for a stomachache," the young woman said.

The sorcier's eyes widened in appreciation at the young beauty before him. Seeing his admiring gaze, she blushed and fluttered her eyelashes.

"I don't believe we have met, madame," the sorcier said to the comely female.

"Mademoiselle," she corrected him with a blush. "No, we have not met, Monsieur le sorcier. I've come down for a visit with my parents. I work as a housemaid in New Orleans."

"I see," said the sorcier, smiling broadly. He gestured for the lovely young woman to step over to his workbench. "Tell me, mademoiselle, what is your opinion of zombies?"

Resources

Ambrose, Kala. *Spirits of New Orleans: Voodoo Curses, Vampire Legends and Cities of the Dead.* Covington, KY: Clerisy Press, 2012.

Ancelet, Barry Jean. *Cajun and Creole Folktales.* Jackson: University Press of Mississippi, 1994.

Asfar, Daniel. *Ghost Stories of Louisiana.* Auburn, WA: Lone Pine Publishing International Inc., 2007.

Asfar, Daniel, and Edrick Thay. *Ghost Stories of America.* Edmonton, AB: Ghost House Books, 2001.

Ashley, Sarah. *Haunted Louisiana: Ghost Stories and Paranormal Activity from the State of Louisiana.* Point Roberts, WA: D&D Publishing, 2013.

Battle, Kemp P. *Great American Folklore.* New York: Doubleday & Company, Inc., 1986.

Botkin, B. A., ed. *A Treasury of Southern Folklore.* New York: Crown Publishers, 1949.

———. *A Treasury of Mississippi River Folklore.* New York: Bonanza Books, 1978.

Boyle, Virginia Frazer. *Devil Tales: Black Americana Folk-Lore.* New York: Harper & Brothers Publishers, 1900.

Brown, Alan. *Stories from the Haunted South.* Jackson: University Press of Mississippi, 2004.

Cable, George W. *Strange True Stories of Louisiana.* Gretna, LA: Pelican Publishing Company, Inc., 1888.

Caskey, James. *The Haunted History of New Orleans: Ghosts of the French Quarter*. Savannah, GA: Subtext Publishing LLC, 2013.

Chamoiseau, Patrick. *Creole Folktales*. New York: New Press, 1994.

Coffin, Tristram P., and Hennig Cohen, eds. *Folklore in America*. New York: Doubleday & AMP, 1966.

———. *Folklore from the Working Folk of America*. New York: Doubleday, 1973.

Cohen, Daniel, and Susan Cohen. *Hauntings & Horrors*. New York: Dutton Children's Books, 2002.

Craughwell, Thomas J. *Urban Legends: 666 Absolutely True Stories that Happened to a Friend . . . of a Friend . . . of a Friend*. New York: Black Dog and Leventhal Publishers, Inc, 2002.

DeLavigne, Jeanne. *Ghost Stories of Old New Orleans*. Baton Rouge: Louisiana State University Press, 2013.

Dorson, R. M. *America in Legend*. New York: Pantheon Books, 1973.

Downer, Deborah L. *Classic American Ghost Stories*. Little Rock, AR: August House Publishers, Inc., 2005

Dwyer, Jeff. *Ghost Hunter's Guide to New Orleans*. Gretna, LA: Pelican Publishing Company, Inc., 2007.

Editors of *Life*. *The* Life *Treasury of American Folklore*. New York: Time, Inc., 1961.

Erdoes, Richard, and Alfonso Ortiz. *American Indian Myths and Legends*. New York: Pantheon Books, 1984.

Flanagan, J. T., and A. P. Hudson. *The American Folk Reader*. New York: A. S. Barnes & Co., 1958.

Fortier, Alcée. *Louisiana Folktales*. Lafayette: University of Louisiana at Lafayette Press, 2011.

Gibbons, Faye. *Hook Moon Night*. New York: Morrow Junior Books, 1997.

Hauck, Dennis William. *Haunted Places: The National Directory*. New York: Penguin Books, 1994.

Holub, Joan. *The Haunted States of America*. New York: Aladdin Paperbacks, 2001.

Klein, Victor C. *New Orleans Ghosts*. Metairie, LA: Lycanthrope Press, 1996.

Leach, M. *The Rainbow Book of American Folk Tales and Legends*. New York: World Publishing Co., 1958.

Leeming, David, and Jake Pagey. *Myths, Legends, & Folktales of America*. New York: Oxford University Press, 1999.

Lindahl, Carl, Maida Owens, and C. Renée Harvison. *Swapping Stories. Folktales from Louisiana*. Jackson: University Press of Mississippi, 1997.

Louisiana Alliance of Witches, ed. *Louisiana Ghost Stories as told by Louisiana Witches*. New Orleans, LA: Left Hand Press, 2012.

Manley, Roger. *Weird Louisiana*. New York: Sterling Publishing Co., Inc., 2010.

Martinez, Raymond J. *Mysterious Marie Laveau Voodoo Queen*. New Orleans, LA: Quaint Press, 2013.

Moore, Elizabeth, and Alice Couvillon. *Louisiana Indian Tales*. Gretna, LA: Pelican Publishing Company, Inc., 1990.

Mott, A. S. *Ghost Stories of America, Vol. II*. Edmonton, AB: Ghost House Books, 2003.

Murphy, Michael. *Fear Dat New Orleans: A Guide to the Voodoo, Vampires, Graveyards & Ghosts of the Crescent City.* New York: Countryman Press, 2015.

Norman, Michael, and Beth Scott. *Historic Haunted America.* New York: Tor Books, 1995.

Pascoe, Jill. *Louisiana's Haunted Plantations.* Gilbert, AZ: Irongate Press, 2004.

Peck, Catherine, ed. *A Treasury of North American Folk Tales.* New York: W. W. Norton, 1998.

Polley, J., ed. *American Folklore and Legend.* New York: Reader's Digest Association, 1978.

———. *The Haunted South.* Columbia: University of South Carolina Press, 1988.

Pustanio, Alyne. *Purloined Stories and Early Tales of Old New Orleans.* Prescott Valley, AZ: Creole Moon Publications, 2013.

———. *Haunting Tales of Old New Orleans, Volume One: History, Legends and Lore.* Self-published. Charleston, SC: Printed by CreateSpace, 2014.

Reneaux, J. J. *Cajun Folktales.* Little Rock, AR: August House, Inc., 1992.

Rule, Leslie. *Coast to Coast Ghosts.* Kansas City, KS: Andrews McMeel Publishing, 2001.

Sillery, Barbara. *The Haunting of Louisiana.* Gretna, LA: Pelican Publishing Company, Inc., 2006.

Skinner, Charles M. *American Myths and Legends*, Vol. 1. Philadelphia: J. B. Lippincott, 1903.

———. *Myths and Legends of Our Own Land*, Vols. 1 & 2. Philadelphia: J. B. Lippincott, 1896.

Smith, Kalila Katherina Smith. *Journey into Darkness . . . Ghosts and Vampires of New Orleans*. New Orleans: DeSimeon Publications, 1997.

Smith, Terry L., and Mark Jean. *Haunted Inns of America*. Birmingham, AL: Crane Hill Publishers, 2003.

Tallant, Robert. *Voodoo in New Orleans*. Gretna, LA: Pelican Publishing Company, Inc., 1946.

Tallant, Robert, and Lyle Saxon. *Gumbo Ya-Ya*. Gretna, LA: Pelican Publishing Company, Inc., 1998.

Thay, Edrick. *Ghost Stories of the Old South*. Edmonton, AB: Ghost House Books, 2003.

Zeitlin, Steven J., Amy J. Kotkin, and Holly Cutting Baker. *A Celebration of American Family Folklore*. New York: Pantheon Books, 1982.

Zepke, Terrance. *Lowcountry Voodoo*. Sarasota, FL: Pineapple Press, Inc., 2009.

About the Author

S. E. Schlosser has been telling stories since she was a child, when games of "let's pretend" quickly built themselves into full-length stories. She created and maintains the website AmericanFolklore.net, where she shares a wealth of stories from all fifty states, some dating back to the origins of America. She lives in Arizona.

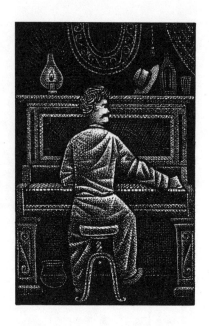

About the Illustrator

Artist Paul Hoffman trained in painting and printmaking. His first extensive illustration work on assignment was in Egypt, drawing ancient wall reliefs for the University of Chicago. His work graces books of many genres—including children's titles, textbooks, short story collections, natural history volumes, and numerous cookbooks. For *Spooky New Orleans*, he employed scratchboard technique and an active imagination.